A Hand Book Of
SCIENTIFIC AND PRACTICAL PALMISTRY

Prof. Dayanand
Institute of Palmistry, New Delhi-48

This book attempts to remove various misconceptions about Palmistry and in a most scientific way explains how the right remedy at the right time can alter one's fortune.

Books For All
Delhi-110052

Distributed by
D.K. Publishers Distributors (P) Ltd.
4834/24, Ansari Road, Darya Ganj,
New Delhi-110002
Phones: 23278584, 23278368, 23261465,
e-mail: dkpd@del3.vsnl.net.in
visit us at: www.dkpd.com

The translation of the original book in Hindi "Palmistry Ke Vaigyanic Aur Vyaavahaarik Sootra"

First Published 2003

ISBN 81-7386-253-2

Published by
Books For All
(an imprint of Low Price Publications)
A-6, Nimri Commercial Centre,
Near Ashok Vihar Phase-IV,
Delhi-110052
Phones: 27401672, 27452453
e-mail: lpp@nde.vsnl.net.in
visit us at: www.lppindia.com

Printed at
D K Fine Art Press P Ltd.
Delhi-110052

PRINTED IN INDIA

Contents

Some Findings of Prof. Dayanand The Founder of Institute of Palmistry

A learned palmist is like a physician. A physician prescribes medicines for a physical ailment but the palmist has to treat the mind which is more difficult than treating the body

*****

Just a physician can understand the functioning of the internal organs of the body through a blood test or other tests, the learned palmist can study the lines on the palm and identify the latent possibilities in a person. Identifying the latent possibilities is the real reading of the past, the present and the future.

*****

Palmistry does not tell you what business or employment you are at any particular time, but it can tell you what you are suited in best.

*****

Fingerprints do not change, but the lines of the palm do. On this basis we can say that we are subject, to some extent, to our destiny, but we can improve our own luck to some extent with our will power.

Preface

I have been interested in learning about the lines on palm right since my adolesence. Psychology has also been my favourite subject right from day one. My first book on psychological problems was published in 1962. Prior to that, I had been regularly contributing my articles etc. to various journals and magazines.

While studying the two subjects I always detected a close and deep relationship between palmistry and psychology, though I could detect the linking clues after working laboriously hand for many years. I will be referring about them all in the coming chapters of this book.

Discerning my so deep interest in palmistry my friends often commented that I was wasting my time and energy in trying to evoke a person's future and past through the study of these lines. They would argue that these lines are actually the creases developed on the child's hand when it remains inside the mother's womb. But I would not agree because I always felt that there is a marked difference in the pattern of the lines etched on each hand. Else, a closed fist should have developed if not identical then at least similar patterns for sure!

While studying the hands of my friends and relations I realised that this branch of knowledge has a definite psychological and physiological basis. However, at that time I had no clues to reveal that basis. But following my deep and continuous study in the subject, its mysteries gradually began to unveil themselves before me. To spread and reveal that knowledge I established in 1989 an Institute of Palmistry. In that I revealed my palmistry-related conclusions and findings before my students and subsequently had my experience and findings in this line also published in the form of many books which contained their very essence in black and white for my readership. The First book among them, entitled : "ALL THE SECRETS OF PALMISTRY", based on my lectures and notes, was the first to hit the stands. My second book on advanced knowledge in palmistry was published with the title "PALMISTRY, HOW TO MASTER IT". The present work is the next link to that series of books on palmistry. Those curious readers well versed in palmistry would appreciate the importance of this book owing to their deep knowledge in the subject.

I have been evoking people's future through the study of the lines in their hands from a long time, much before the establishment of the Institute of Palmistry. *I was assisted in it by my daughter* ***Nisha***, who also gained some practical experience in this line in my company.

Some hands have the lines revealing the future of the person quite clearly while some are really very complicated hands. Looking at them **Nisha** used to throw probing questions at me which often *churned* my knowledge deeply to let me reveal their indications with no ambiquity.

Today I am putting this book along with my mental journey into this field before you. During this process my belief in the efficacy of palmistry divining people's future became firmer and firmer and today I can say with full conviction that palmistry is a totally scientific study.

In this book I have also mentioned those questions which Nisha asked during our study sessions. It is while answering those questions that my doubts were also cleared and my conclusions kept on becoming more and more clear.

It is hoped that this book will help resolve many mysterious facts concerning palmistry and shall open new vistas for further research to let palmistry break out of the cover of occultism and get established as a full-fledged science.

Dayanand
W-21, Greater Kailash – I
New Delhi - 110048

BASIC INFORMATION ABOUT THE PALM

Before delving deep into scientific aspect of the palmistry; here is some basic information about the subject.

The shape and size of the thumb, fingers and the different areas of the palm depict the basic nature of the person and the lines of the palm tell about the possible ups and downs in the life of the native.

Peculiarities of Fingers and Mounts

The Thumb

It depicts the intelligence and discretion of the native.

The space between the base of thumb and the wrist is called the **Mount of Venus** (See fig. *A-1*). Mount of Venus reveals about physical vitality of a person and is responsible for the relations between man and woman. These relations include emotion of sympathy, sex etc.

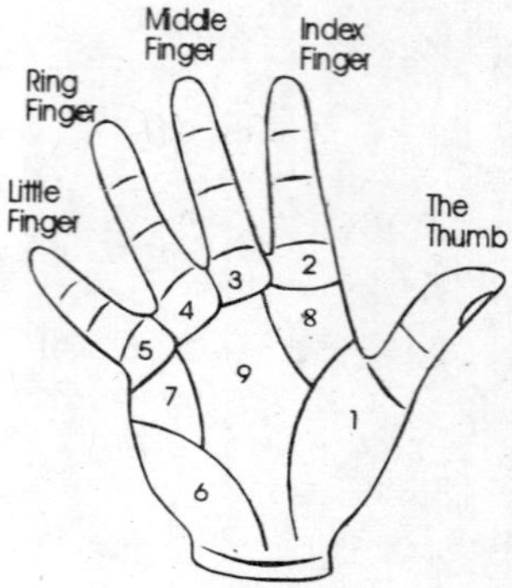

Fig. A

The finger adjacent to the Thumb called the **Index Finger**. The area just below the Index Finger is known as the **Mount of Jupiter** (See fig. *A*-2).

Index finger and the Mount of Jupiter reveal about the degree of egoistic tendency, the sense of loyalty and ambition of the native.

The next finger adjacent to the Index finger is generally longer than the other fingers. It is called the **Middle Finger** and area just below the Middle Finger is known as the **Mount of Saturn**. (See fig. *A-3*).

The Middle Finger and the Mount of Saturn depict the extent of the sobriety and the introversion in the personality.

The third finger next to the Middle Finger, is known as the **Ring Finger**. A small space below the Ring Finger is known the **Mount of Sun** (See fig. *A-4*). The Ring finger and the Mount of Sun represent the extroversive capacity of the person.,

Next to the Ring Finger, the fourth finger is generally smaller than all other fingers. It is called the Little Finger. The space below the **Little Finger** is known as the **Mount of Mercury**. (See fig. *A-5*)

The little Finger and the Mount of Mercury tells about the restlessness and practical approach, business acumen and the worldliwiseness of the person.

The space opposite the Mount of Venus and above the wrist is connected with the imagination and love for change in a person. This space is known as the **Mount of Moon or Luna**. (See fog. *A-6*)

A small space above the Mount of Moon and below the Mount of Mercury (See fig. *A-7*) is responsible for the capacity of patience and endurance in the person.

Old name of this space was **Upper Mars**, but the author has named this space due to its peculiarity, as the Mount of **Defensive Mars**.

The small space opposite to the Defensive Mars and below the Mount of Jupiter is responsible for the aggressive tendency in the person (See fig. *A-8*). Old name of this space is **Lower Mars**, but the author has named this space in his books as the **Mount of Aggressive Mars** due to its peculiar characteristics.

The middle portion of the palm, which is the centre of all Mounts, tells about the enterprising capability of the person and is called the **Plain of Mars** (See fig. *A-9*)

The lines

With regard to the lines of the palm, some lines already exist on the human palm at the time of birth. These are called **Main Lines**. Some lines are formed by the sub conscious mind by its being continuously active in one direction. These are called **Secondary Lines**. Some lines keep on appearing and disappearing from time to time. They reflect the activeness of the subconscious mind and are called **Influence Lines**.

The Main Lines

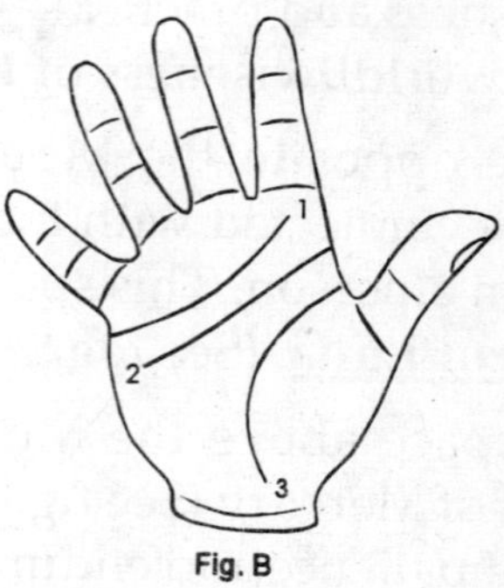

Fig. B

See these three main lines in the Figure B. Out of these, the upper horizontal Line near the base of the fingers is popularly known as the **Line of Heart**. (Fig. *B-1*) This details about the emotion of love, hate, jealously etc. are revealed from the Line of Heart.

Lower horizontal line is popularly known as the **Line of Head** (Fig. *B-2*). This line tells about the quantum of practical aspect and thinking capability of a person.

Apart from these two lines; a semi circularly round shaped line is found on all the palms which runs below the Mount of Jupiter and goes up to the wrist and is popularly known as the **Line of Life**. (See fig. *B-3*). It tells about physical health and family of the person.

The Secondary Lines

Secondary Lines are said to be those lines which are formed by the electric current emanating from some centers of the brain. They run from wrist towards fingers. Name of these Lines are, Line of Saturn, Line of Sun, Line of Mercury. (See fig. C)

Line of Saturn (See fig. *C-1*)

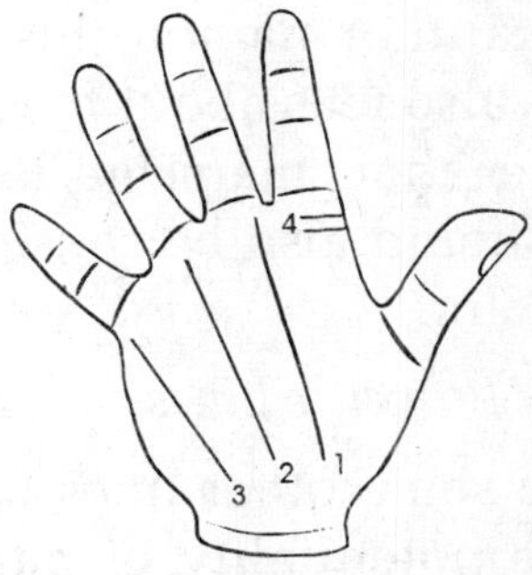

Fig. C

It emerges near the wrist or Mount of Moon or Mount of Venus and goes to the Mount of Saturn. This line tells about the person's materialistic attitude, like his approach towards career, property, business etc.

Line of Sun (See fig. *C-2*)

This is supporting line to the Line of Saturn and ensures success to the endeavours of the person. It emerges near the wrist or middle of palm and goes to the Mount of Sun.

Line of Mercury (See fig. *C-3*)

Old palmists have considered this line to be the Line of Health or Line of Liver (Hepatica) but the author found it by his experience to be a line showing of intelligence of the person. It tells about the quality of nervous system. Its origin may be Mount of Venus or Mount of Luna or Middle of the palm. Its destination is Mount of Mercury.

So called Line of Marriage (See fig. *C-4*)

This is another important line which is found almost on all the hands is named as Line of Association or Line of Marriage. But according to the author's experience this line/s does not give satisfactorily answer to the questions regarding love, marriage and divorce. So the author named this line (s) a Line of Sexuality as this also tells about the sexual vitality of a person. To answer about marriage, love etc. Line of Sun, Line of Saturn should also be considered for accurate reading of the palm.

Some supporting / Influence Lines

There are some other lines found on the palm which show the potentiality of particular Mount or which act as the supporting lines of some main or secondary lines. Some of them are given below:

Lines of Intuition

It is like a bridges between Mount of Moon and Mount of Mercury. Inherent power of nervous system surplus the range of imagination define one's intuitive capacity. (See fig. *D-1*)

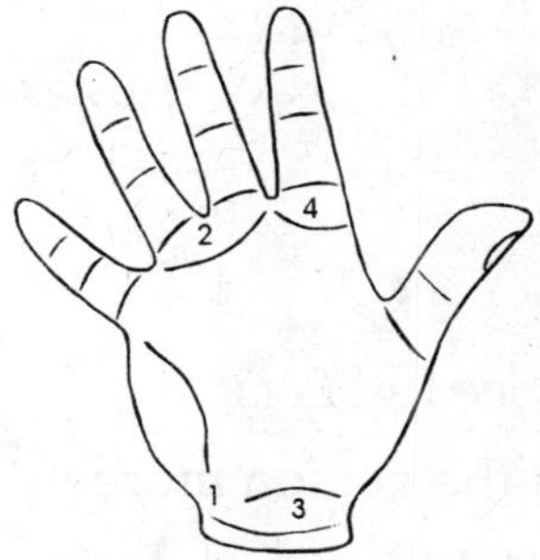

Fig. D

Girdle of Venus (See fig. *D*-2)

It has no connection with the Mount of Venus. It is supporting Line of Heart and reveals the person's extra sensitivity.

Via Lasciva (See fig. *D*-3)

It is the bridge between Mount of Moon and the Mount of Venus. Sexuality and imagination make a person more sensuous, if it is found on a heavy hand; the same combination makes the person addicted to drugs and alcoholic drinks if it is found on a thin hand.

Ring of Soloman (See fig. *D*-4)

It enhances characteristics of Jupiter and as a result, the person becomes more egoistic.

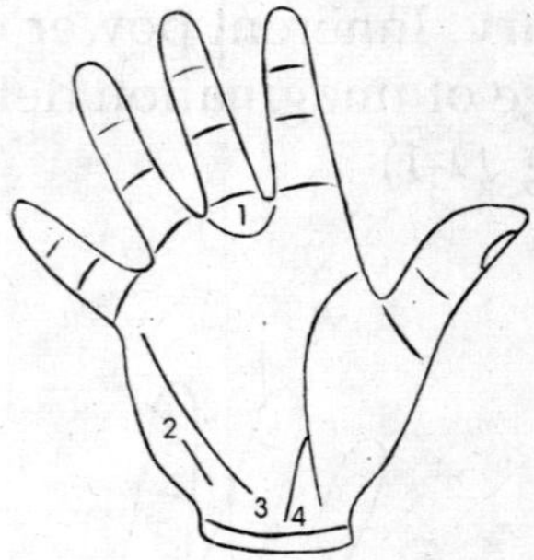

Fig. E

Ring of Saturn (See fig. *E-1*)

It makes the person more introvert.

Mount of Moon and Mount of Mercury, both make a person restless and eager for change. So the vertical line from wrist to both the Mounts (See fig. *E-2 & 3*) or from Line of Life to Mount of Moon (See fig. *E-4*) show the tendency to undertake more journeys. These are called **Travel Lines**.

All other small lines which are called *Influence Lines* reveal more about the potency of the Mount on which they appear.

Part - I

The Scientific Formulae

Chapter I

THE SCIENTIFIC BASIS OF THE LINES ON THE PALM

Once I was busy in my study in a library, collecting material for writing a book on psychology. There, in a book on physiology, I happened to come across a figure of the 'Somatosensory Area' of the human brain. In that figure there was much representation of a person's face in his brain's chart. After that there was a big area marked for a person's hands and fingers. That picture strengthened my belief that there is a deep relationship between a person's hand and his brain. I had published this figure in my book : "ALL THE SECRETS OF PALMISTRY" which is given in this book as well at the relevant place.

Thereafter, in 1978 another vital fact unveiled itself before me when I went to a printing press to give the proofs of my yet another book. It further deepened my interest in this knowledge. I happened to find there a roller used for bringing out the proofs. Sheer curiosity made me take my palm's print with that roller. It had the print of my lines and the fingers very clearly etched on it. Putting my name and the date of that day on that palm print, I put it in a cupboard, reaching back home. My other pressing engagements almost made me forget about that print which kept on lying buried under the mound of the files.

It was almost after a full decade that I happened to put my hand accidentally on that palm-print while cleaning my old files. When I compared that palm-print of mine with my live-palm I found many fresh lines emerging while some of the old ones had faded or deepened also [See *Fig.1*] my palm-print taken in 1978.

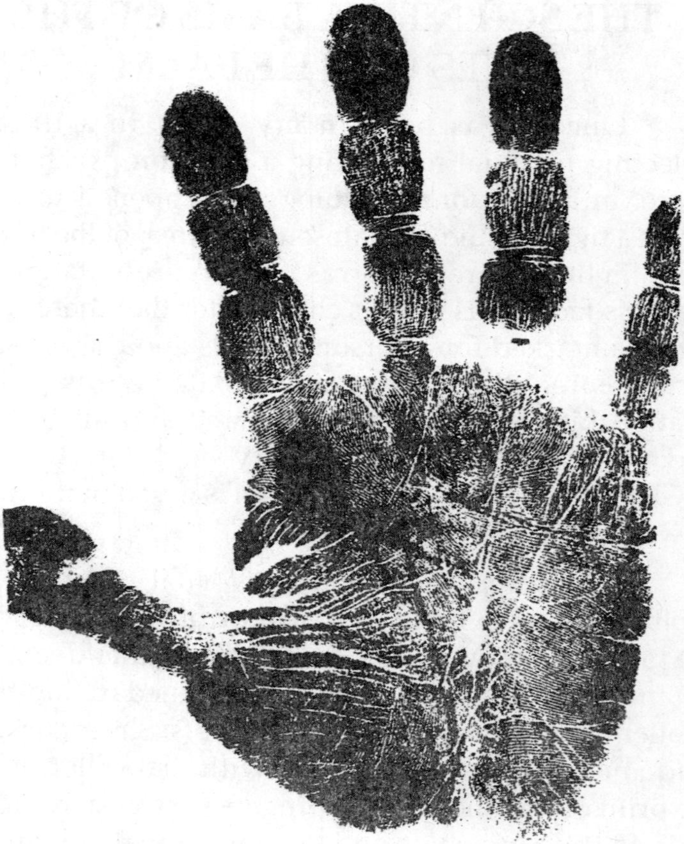

Fig. 1: Author's right hand's palm print taken in 1978

At that time I was mentally very calm. But the palm-print taken in 1988 (*Fig.2*) reveals my disturbed mental state. During that phase I was very upset with many problems.

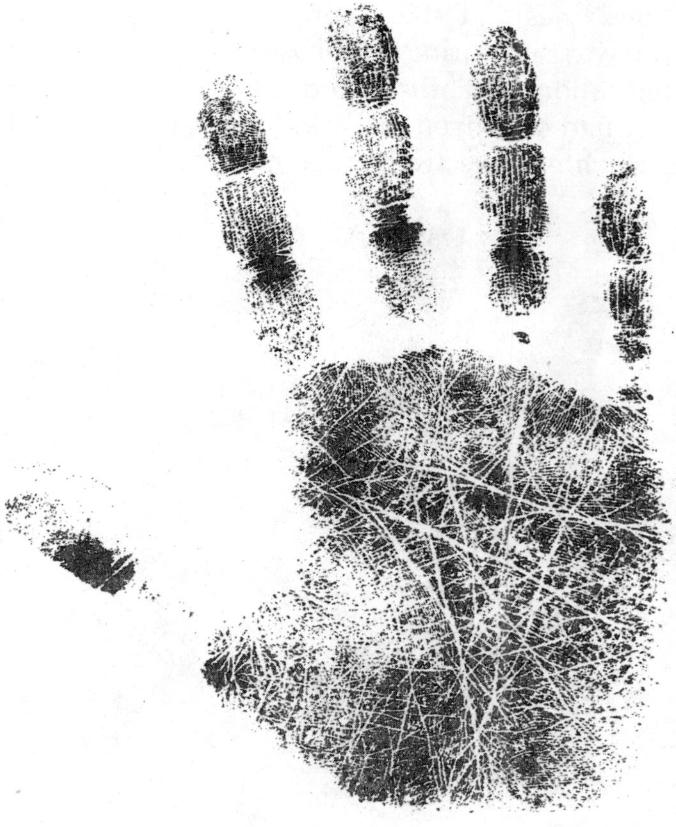

Fig. 2: Author's right hand's palm print taken in 1988

I was, in fact, amazed to notice this marked change in my lines. Until that time my firm belief was the lines of palm reveal the scrawl of Destiny. Although that inscription is generally held immutable, the changes occuring on my lines created a doubt in my mind. I deduced that if these lines reveal one's fortune it means one's fate is also quite changeable. With this thought in 1991 I again took a fresh print of my palm [See *Fig.3*]. This reveals the disappearnce of many superfluous lines and sharpening of the major lines. The reason was that during this phase through the *Dhyan Yoga* (Meditation) and other mind-relaxing practices or *Sadhanas,* I had stabilized my mind a great deal; I had clarified my life's objectives much more specifically.

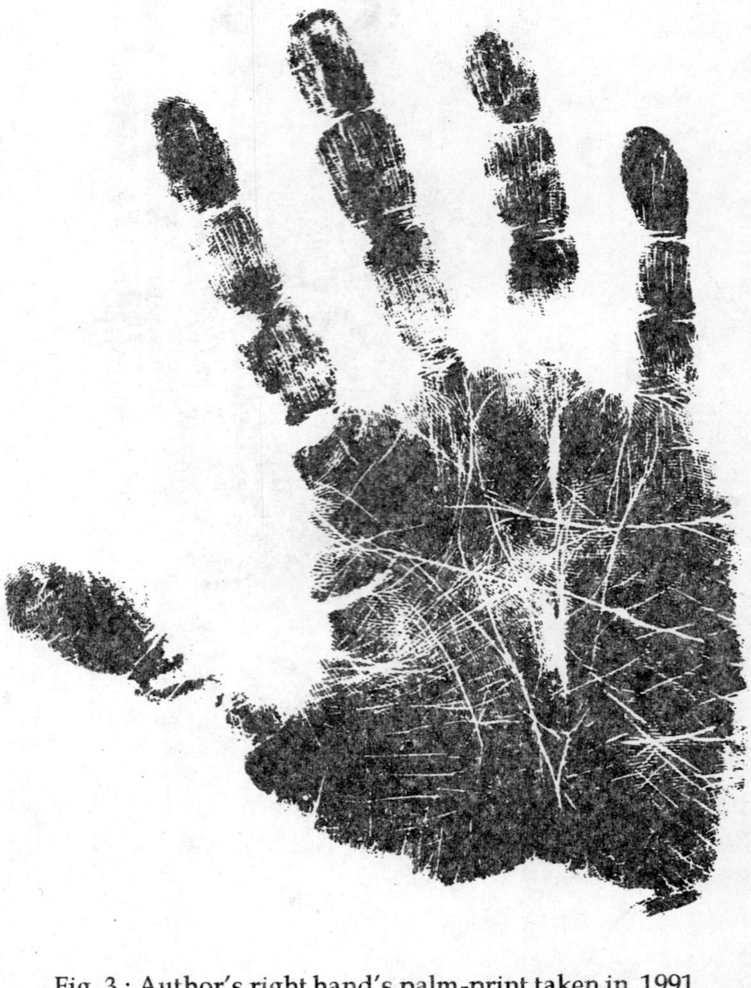

Fig. 3 : Author's right hand's palm-print taken in 1991

It was this changeability of the palm-lines that inspired me to dive deep into this knowledge. Thereafter I collected palm-prints of my many friends and relations. When I compared their old palm-prints with the new ones I found some had the lines markedly changed, while most of the person's lines failed to register any noticeable change.

When I peeped deep into their life-patterns, I found that those who took life with equanimity had almost no change in their palm-lines. But those with a sensitive nature and reacted deeply to every situation had the marked change in their lines, particularly on their active hand. Active hand means the hand with which we write. Concluding my all study and experience in this field I can say with conviction that the lines on our palms reveal the inscription of the unconscious mind. It is through that inscription the unconscious mind uses the brain as its manifesting instrument.

Nisha : You call lines on the palm to be symbolising the inscription of the unconscious mind and deem brain to be an instrument of the same mind. Please elaborate on the distinction of the mind, the unconscious mind and the brain for my benefit.

Answer : The Indian scriptures have copiously referred to about the mind of a person. In the ninth *Shloka* of the 15th canto of '*Srimadbhagwat Gita*' Lord Krishna says it is the *Jivatma* (individual soul) which uses mind (*Munn*) as the medium to enjoy all sensory delights through various media of perception like ear, eye, skin, tongue and nose.

Nisha : Please enlighten me about the seat of mind inside the body.

Answer : The study of the Indian scriptures revels a clue to answer this question. Whichever sensory organ's perception the mind focuses on, it is dwelling in that perception fully that the mind enjoys all feelings of grief and happiness through that sense only. It is also said that the calm and the inactive stage of mind is what we know by *'Antah Karand'* or the state of inner self. The active stage of that inner sense is the mind *munn*. This means that mind does not have a fixed or definite seat in a body. Implicatly it also means that it is the mind which pervade the entire body.

Although the modern psychology fails to determine the fixed seat or place of the mind inside the body, it imagines the mind having three levels :

1. The Conscious Mind
2. The Subconscious Mind
3. The Unconscious Mind

The functions of these three levels are divided the following ways :

1. In the awakened state the conscious mind feels the sensation of pleasure or pain.

2. The Subconscious mind conducts the dreams or the actions committed on that stage of dream.

3. The deepest level is the Unconscious mind which contains our ancestors' desires and the possibilities of their achievements in future. Psychology calls them desires and the possibilities as the basic instincts. The theory of genes attribute those desires and their possibility of achievements to the genes that we inherit from our ancestors.

Modern psychology often compares the mind with a floating ice-berg on the sea which is normally only *1/10th* out of the sea's surface. What is visible is the conscious mind. The *9/10th* part of it, hidden below the surface, contains the subconscious and the unconscious mind. The psychologists and the psychiatrists are trying to reveal that invisible part through their separate ways and methods which include hypnotism and psychoanalysis.

The ancient Indian *Tantra Vidya* shows a miracle by activating the boundless power of the unconscious mind. The adepts and experts by going into the *Yoga Samadhi* (meditative trance) also teach concentrating the unconscious mind's power to make the performer accomplish extra-ordinary feats. In colloquial parlance the expertise in the having such trances to acquire special powers are called the *'Yoga Siddhi'* (acquiring mireculous powers through Yoga).

Now I revert to the brain. The modern psychology has discovered the centres (areas) of the five sensory organs in the brain. They are given below :

1. Visual Area
2. Auditory Area
3. Olfactory Area
4. Gustatory Area
5. Somatosensory Area

The modern physiology, however, has failed to identify the seat of the mind in the brain so far.

The somatosensory center records the motion of touch on the skin. It analyses whether the touch is hot or cold, hard or soft but its reaction in the mind, or which part of the brain records it and how, is not known so far to the modern psychology.

Nisha : Please elaborate on this point.

Answer : A woman undergoes mentally different experiences when her breast is touched by her new-born child or by her lover or husband. You record different experience when your skin is touched by a flower or by a lizard. So the actual center of recording these experiences is the mind whose specific seat could not be searched so far in the body.

The modern physiology which has searched the center in the brain conducting the activities of the motor organs or sensory organs has failed to pin point that part in the brain which regulates the ego sense. Those centers have not yet been found in the brain whose activities make a person introvert or extrovert; magnanimous (large hearted) or selfish, day dreamer or practical. But Palmistry draws our attention to those centers quite specifically.

By studying the developed or underdeveloped mounts on the palm, the length of the fingers, a palmist can reveal about the mental powers of the person. For instance, the mount of Mercury or the size of the little finger can reveal a person's intelligence or worldliwiseness . The mount of the moon gives a clue to the person's imaginative power. But what are those centers in the body which regulate or conduct the person's worldliwiseness or imagination is not known even to him. But catching the clues from the symptoms which reveal on the palm we are trying to reach up to the very conducting centers of these mental faculties. According to our hypothesis those relate to the mind and the brain. The mind and the brain also play an important role in the origin of the lines on the palm.

Nisha : Please elaborate on this hypothesis and reveal its connection with science.

__Answer__ : The hypothesis is the seed, while science reflects its manifestation. It is, however, not necessary that every hypothesis attains the status of science but this cannot be denied that very scientific conclusion has its basis in some hypothesis. When the constant experimentation and testing process is continued on the basis of that hypothesis we reach to its eventual vindication (proof) which is then hailed as the scientific truth.

__Nisha__ : Would you please explain your this tense observation with the help of some examples ?

__Answer__ : The earth's gravitational pull is now as established scientific truth. This is the result of the hypothesis made by a British Scientist, Newton, about 400 years ago.

Newton saw an apple falling on the ground from its tree. This observation flashed an idea in his mind as to why this apple had fallen only on the earth? Why didn't it go skywards the moment it was broken away from the tree ?

Of course any common-man would term this thought of Newton as an outcome of insanity because every dropped thing comes down from above. The same way the apple fell on to the ground from its tree. What was a big surprise in it ? But Newton's science-oriented wisdom was seeing the manifestation of the principle of the force of gravitation of the earth in this event.

Subsequently, the scientific tests conclusively proved that every planet has its distinct gravitational pull which pulls every thing to itself coming in its range. Now, a student with elementary knowledge of astronomy knows that the earth's gravitational pull is more than that of the moon but less than that of Jupiter and that balanced by each planet's gravitational force all satellite, planets, stars and constellation move around their fixed orbits.

This principle of the gravitational pull must have been known to India's ancient astronomers. Hence they could calculate the speed of various planets and stars even centuries before. However, the credit for revealing this principle of gravitation to the modern world goes to Newton. It is the result of this major discovery that now space-ships could be sent to various stars and planets. Nevertheless, the point from which Newton made this observations was just a hypothesis.

Nisha : You seem inclined to prove your point by referring to various hypothesis made in physics. But our subject is man who is not a dead material but a living being. Give as example of some living being to prove your point.

Answer : The theory of genes is now an established fact of science. Its use in genetic engineering has resulted in our procuring novel seeds of the herbs and vegetation; those hens which now hatch many more eggs than they did earlier. The DNA test has made it possible now to identify the unknown parents. The clone of sheep has already been developed and the modern man is now quite capable to develop his own clone.

This basic seed of modern science is, in fact, based upon our old beliefs. For many generation we know that a person inherits his ancestors' complexion, shape, size and habits. It is on this basis when we think of keeping a dog we try to decipher its breed. Before laying our stake on any horse in the horse-race we study the pedigree-chart of that horse. However, the question relating to deciphering the clues to this ancestral similarity continuing for generations was what had been troubling the scientists for a long time. It is their hard toil in this field that led to the revelation of the genes theory most.

So this genes' theory is also the final fruction of a mere hypothesis which first flashed in the mind of a Bishap Mendel of Marovia in Checkoslovakia in the 19th century.

While planting peas in the field Mandel observed that in a typical set order, one grain of it was fatter than other grains of a particular plant. Conversely, one grain of every pea was smaller than others in a set pattern. Why was it so? In order to reach up to the answer to this 'why', Mandel made experiments on a variety of plants. Subsequently, other scientists repeated those experiments on the living beings which Mandel had conducted on herbs and plants. It is the end-result of that collective endeavour that we have the established gene's theory before us now.

Nevertheless it is simpler to vindicate the hypothesis made in the field of Physics, Chemistry or genetics through various experiments linked with our mind. Because, the mind is not the name of any particular limb of our body and it has no fixed place in our body as well.

In psychology it is this very fact that has been impressed upon the people by giving the example of ice-berg, which compare its revealed view with the conscious and unrevealed; with the sub-conscious and unconscious states of the mind. But, the mind, in fact, is not an ice-berg. It is something which is beyond the sensory perception but we are helpless to explain it with the example of a matter.

Nisha : I realise this helplessness expressed by you. Now, you call the lines on the palm as the inscription made by our unconscious mind. But the question is : how can our unconscious mind know the past and future about which we ourselves are not knowingly conscious ?

Answer : In order to answer this question, I must repeat whatever I have already said. Modern psychology says, it is in the deep recess of our mind that our basic instincts lie hidden . According to our ancient Indian belief these are our *Karmas* accumulated over past many lives which are called *Sanskar*. However, both coincide that these get accumulated in our past only. It is these past-accumulated instincts that showed in the seed form our present and future instincts. Any botanist, with his experience can predict about a plant or a tree after studying its seed. Deem the unconscious to be representing the seed which does not know itself as to how it is likely to grow or what it may eventually become.

Nisha : How can you be so sure about the seed not knowing about its eventual form. Please give your argument to clarify your this statement.

Answer : By giving an example of a human infant I hope to satisfy your curiosity. As soon as a man with common sense sees the infant's urinary organ he can tell whether it would have beard and mustaches or will have breasts, even when that infant may not be aware of these possibilities. The infant is a live being and naturally more aware than the seed of a tree.

In order to clarify our point more specifically we say that an ordinary person may not be aware as to what is the basic reason behind these developments occuring in a human body as it gains youth. But some one versed in the knowledge of harmonal secretions can easily tell that the harmone called Androgen is responsible for causing these changes in youth in a male body and Estrogen causes such changes in a female body at that stage – like development of breasts etc.

Although this knowledge about the harmones has only been gained only in last century, for millennia together male heifers have continued to be castrated to get a bull from a bison.

The same way, for millennium together, the palmists have been studying hands to predict the future and reveal the past of the people. But, now, it is that we are trying to unearth the basic theory and secret to know as to how those symptoms on the hand can reveal one's life.

In fact, the whole map of our life remains hidden in our unconscious mind in the seminal form called *Sanskaras*. Predicting the future by looking only at the said before it turns into a full grown tree with leaves and fruits making prophesy about one's life.

There are, however, many methods of making such prophesies. One of them is astrology : by studying the movement of the planets and constellations. Doing the same by studying the symptoms on the hand - lines and mounts and other signs on the palm, is palmistry. At present, confining our hypothesis to this, second, method only, we are delving deeper into this subject.

Generally; palmistry is deemed to be a secret or occult science. We predict one's future by studying the lines in conformity with only our bookish knowledge and puke it out as it is, while our firm belief is that the lines on the palm and other symptoms are the consequence of the activities that take place in those centers in our brain in whose conduction our mind plays a significant role.

It is by studying the lines on the hand that we endeavour to reach the basic spurce of them. Any success in this endeavour will surely place palmistry on the pedestal of a scientific knowledge though it would be closer to psychology than physiology or the physics of the body.

Chapter II

THE RELATION BETWEEN THE BRAIN AND THE SYMPTOMS ON THE HAND

The mounts on the palm, texture of the skin, shape of the hand and fingers reveal a person's basic nature. And the basic nature of a person affects its every action and every relationship. In turn, those good or bad relations also cast their impact on the person's fate also.

Most of the books on palmistry try to reveal the effect of those symptoms but not the basic cause behind them.

In our book : "All The Secrets Of Palmistry" in the chapter dealing with the nails we have stated that those with smaller nails regard their beliefs as being most proper and the best. In the chapter dealing with the skin we have stated that persons with hard skin lack flexibility in their thought while those who have more whorls on their palm do not like to compromise on their decision.

If a person happens to be placed in a high position, these very qualities reveal his firm resolves. However, lauding such firm resolves as an essential quality of man may make that person grow all the more arrogant and this arrogance can arrest his progress.

But when a person with these qualities be lowly placed he would be called adamant. Those above him may not like his firm resolves. This may reduce the chances of his promotion as well. He may start feeling as if every body is against him. But he or she refuses to learn as to why people act this way.

No matter whether the relations be between the husband and wife, between the master and servant or between the trader and his customer, the person's basic nature shows it good or bad impact in every relationship.

Nisha : Any other example ?

Answer : Those with well developed Mount of Jupiter seek respect and honour. One with well developed aggressive Mars (mount) would not bow or succumb before anyone; he or she will always try to subdue others. In case he or she is compelled to succumb, this compulsion would escalate his or her tension. Those with longer ring finger take hasty decisions or are prone to taking risks. The lines of hand will reveal whether their taking risk or hasty decision affect their life favourably or adversely. The same way other mounts or fingers show their effect. Hence before revealing the effects of the lines it is necessary to consider the mounts and the fingers which tell of the person's basic nature.

Nisha : What is the scientific basis concerning the basic nature?

Answer : The existing physiological studies give a suggestion about the centers controlling the thumb and fingers. One Figure of the brain's somatosensory area has already been given in our book : 'All The Secrets Of Palmistry'. Now with a fraction of that Figure we put forth our hypothesis. This Figure is made on the basis of the chart given in a book HUMAN PHYSIOLOGY part two published in Russia and edited by E.B. Babsky.(See Fig. *No. 4*)

This Figure shows the areas concerning the palm and the fingers which don't exist in the given form but indicate toward the possibility they would be in.

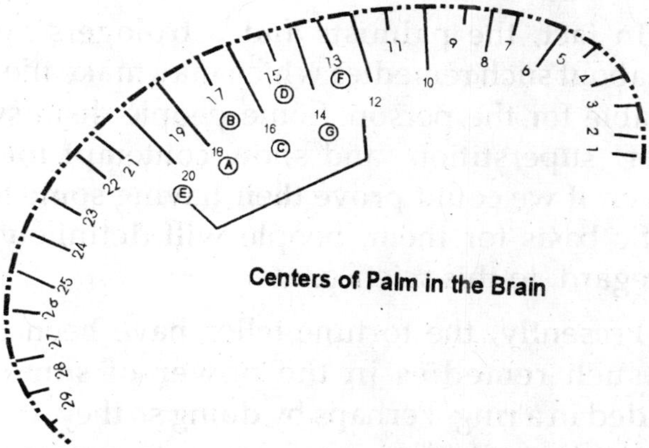

Fig. 4

The chart (Centres of Palm in the Brain)

The brain housed in the skill is the most complicated part of the human body. It is rather impossible to clearly depict all the centers regulating the hand. On the basis of the indication shown in the Figure an endeavour could be made to identify the centers regulating the person's nature.

Nisha : What is the advantage of seeking the centers regulating the person's basic nature ?

Answer: He who consults a palmist doesn't do so with the intention of only knowing about his future. He also wants to know about the remedies to be employed to make his future favourable should it be showing potential adversity. In case he is not told about such remedies, in the deep apprehension of facing an adverse future, he might commit even a most untoward act.

In case we are able to pin-point the basic cause of his potential adversity, it would be quite possible for us to suggest an effective anti-dote for it.

In fact, the palmists and astrologers keep on telling about such remedies which may make the future favourable for the person. Some people dismiss them as sheer superstition and show contempt for them. However, if we could prove their having some logical, scientific basis for them, people will definitely show more regard to this science.

Presently, the fortune-teller have been talking about such remedies in the power of some gems embedded in a ring. Perhaps by doing so they are rather inadvertently providing extra power to certain centers of the brain. This is nothing but just groping in the dark. If we succeed in finding the right centers in the brain controlling the various mounts and lines on the palm, may be, we succeed in taking this knowledge out from, realm of occultism or the so called 'black-knowledge'.

<u>Nisha</u> : **If according to your hypothesis, a fortune-teller, by charging the brain-relevant centers, succeeds in influencing the native's fate, won't he be intervening in the work of God ? Is it possible to alter one's *Sanskars* accumulated through a series of past lives(*Poorva Janam*)?**

<u>**Answer**</u> : If my eye-sight is weak, I must use the powered spects. If my one relation's kidney is not working properly, he has to survive through frequent dialysis. I mean, taking the help of medicines during

illness; using clutches when my legs are not strong enough or conceiving through the test-tube technique should also be considered to be an intervention in God's work, in that case.

What the medicines achieve at the physical level, the same is attained by the spiritual remedies at the mind's level. Hence these remedies should be taken as no different then using the medicines to keep the body fit.

Man is an active being. He has best brain endowed by God to any living species. By applying his brain in the right direction, surely he can improve his future. It is a good fortune-teller's job to render the right advice at right time.

Now before telling about the fingers and various mounts on the palm we are showing the Fig. of the mounts on the palm and of the fingers.

We start this process by discussing the mounts at the base of first finger and the finger itself.

<u>*The First Finger And The Mount Of Jupiter*</u>

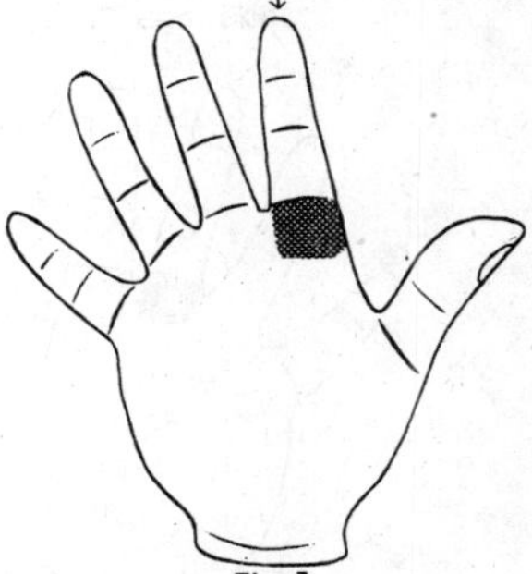

Fig. 5

The essential fact about this finger and the mount– by modern palmistrical lexicon – is that both indicate to the native having leadership qualities and ambition (See *Fig. 5*). Here it needs to be clarified that having the ambition and the leadership qualities and actually achieving the same are two different propositions. In order to have this desire fulfilled one must have other conducive symptoms on the palm as well.

Normally, the persons who come to us for showing their hands have well developed Mount of Jupiter in general. They feel constrained by the problems and have strong desire to get honour and renown. They find it difficult to bow before any one. Little blow on their ego leads to invariably tensions and depression.

The mind center controlling the ego sense of the person is shown at 'A' part in the Fig.number 4. In fact, that shows its most possible placement. It is because this part covers the first finger which is deemed to be the extension of the Jupiter Mount or vice-versa.

Now we concentrate on the middle finger and at the Mount of Saturn at its base.

The Middle Finger And The Mount Of Saturn

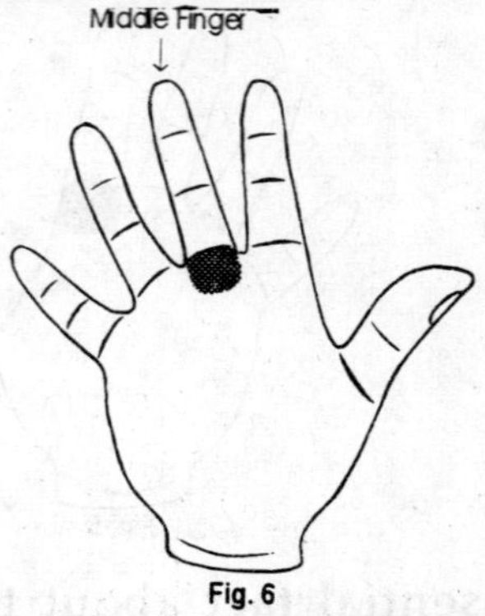

Fig. 6

Normally the Mount of Saturn is depressed but the middle finger connected with this mount is the longest among all fingers. (See *Fig.No. 6*). For this reason even the depressed Mount of Saturn shows the effect of a well developed mount. In case, with this long finger, if the mount is also well developed, the effect of Saturn is twicely accentuated.

Those with predominant Saturn have their nerve-system well developed, although from physical point of view they may be weak. The prominent features of such a personality are sobriety, introversiveness and stability in character. Normally the nature with Saturn's predominiance has knotty fingers which reveal his advanced capacity to analyses. Such a person never takes decision in an emotional vein but after weighing the pros and cons well. Other symptoms on the palm and lines indicate his trend of thinking.

The persons with dominant Saturn love loneliness and shun crowd. Always remaining lost in their work and inching towards their aim is their style. They don't sink their money in flamboyant ventures but always save it for the rainy day. They don't like to put their money in speculation but invest in solid organisation to ensure their getting a fixed and steady income. Instead of investing in property (particularly landed property or real estate) they love to invest their money in such a way as would fetch them steady interest.

They are generally quiet and very reluctant to reveal their personal weal or woe. It is often difficult to fathom their mind. Their friend's circle is invariably small but they always prove to be a very faithful friend.

Other conducive symptoms on their palm bring about distinct change in their outward behaviour. The one with Saturn is predominance, associated with other favourable signs and symptoms on the palm make them inventors, planners and mathematicians. Unfavourable or inauspicious symptoms make them conspirators, pervented, whimsical and suspicious by nature. If the center of their sobriety and introvert nature is to be found, the possibility of its placement would be near the middle finger area which is shown in '*B*' part of the Fig.number 4.

The Ring Finger And The Mount of Sun

This finger reveals about the person's extrovert nature and the tendency to take the risk as well. The Mount of Sun is located at this finger's base. (See *Fig.No. 7*) Those with long ring fingers and developed Mount of Sun are called the Sun dominant personalities. Normally the Mount of Sun is found to be rather depressed. If there be a vertical line on this mount, it should be deemed as well developed. Two vertical lines indicate over developed Mount of Sun. However, if there be more than two vertical lines, they lessen this mount's potency. Such a person cannot concentrate on his one aim, hence is deprived of success.

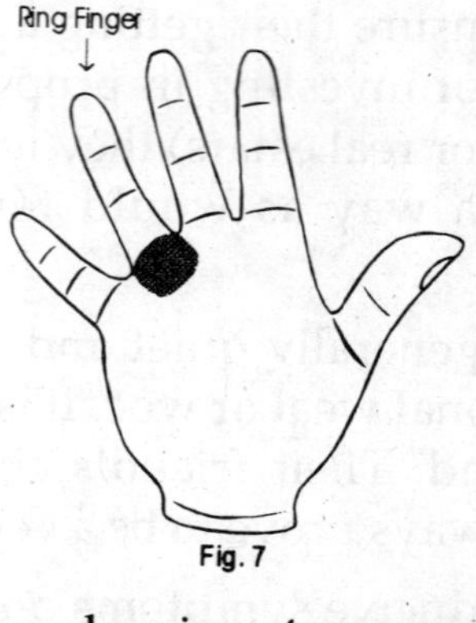

Fig. 7

But the sun dominant persons are generally open-hearted being. They don't hide their feelings. Their friend-circle is always big. If other conducive symptoms be present on the palm they become celebrities. They can suffer poverty or scarcity owing to maintain their "show". If inauspicious symptoms be present on the palm, their fame give way to even notoriety.

If the center for the person's extrovertness is to be sought, the base of the ring finger shown at 'C' in Fig.4 should be concentrated upon.

The Little Finger And The Mount of Mercury

This little finger and the Mount of Mercury at its base give out the nature's intelligence or prudence, opportunistic bent of mind and the ability to impress by their speech. (See *Fig. No. 8*)

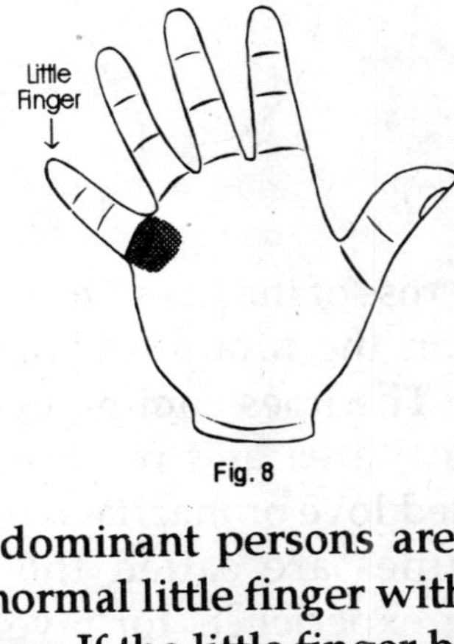

Fig. 8

Mercury dominant persons are those that have longer than the normal little finger with well developed Mount of Mercury. If the little finger be thick, also with its being longer than the normal size, the qualities of Mercury get accentuated. Even this finger be a little crook, it augments the qualities associated with Mercury.

The Mercury-dominated persons have over developed nervous system. Although this may also be so with the Saturn-dominated persons, the difference is while the Mercury-dominated persons are extrovert, those with Saturn-domination are generally introvert. While the Saturn-dominated persons are of stable nature, the Mercury dominated one even desire change. They constantly try to alter their place of work, their job and their business as well. Conducive (or auspicious) symptoms on the palm make them successful but non-conducive (or inauspicious) symptoms may often bring infamy to their name.

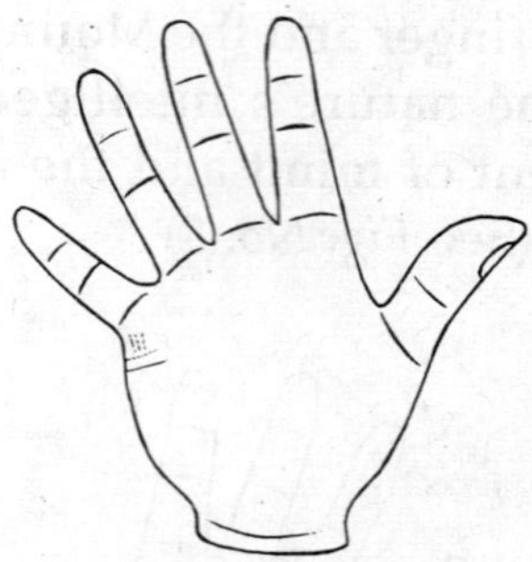

Fig. 8a

The criss-cross of the lines (vertical or horizontal) and capillaries on the Mount of Mercury still need further research. The lines coming even from outside palm (percussion) area and reaching this Mount of Mercury are called love or marriage lines. The vertical lines on these lines are called the progeny lines. According to our experience, for revealing the details of one's love-life, the Mount of Venus, the Mount of Luna, The Saturn Line and the Heart Line should be considered upon. The Mount of Venus also gives much information about one's progeny whose details we shall mention in the coming chapter.

The Western Palmists call the vertical lines on the Mercury Mount as the Medical Stigma. In our view these lines indicate towards the direction of research to be undertaken. It may be towards the medical field, business, criminology, domestic work, or anything like these fields. If the center of self-preservation or self-protection instinct or selfish nature in the brain is to be sought, it may be around part *'D'* in the Fig.No. 4, which also regulates the activities of the little finger.

The Thumb And The Mount of Venus

The position of the thumb is totally different from that of the fingers. While the four fingers can be tilted towards the wrist, the thumb towards the fingers. It is because of this different position of the thumb that we can close our fist. Both fingers and the thumb are used to firmly hold any object.

However, this is not the sole use of the thumb. In palmistry it represents one's prudence. On one end of the palm there is the thumb while on the other the little finger. Although the little finger also symbolises prudence but its attributes are closer to cunningness and smartness. Whereas, the thumb shows one's power of discernment, to distinguish between what is proper and what is improper.

Longer than the normal thumb indicates the dictatorial mentality. Other conducive or auspicious symptoms on the hand help one succeed as a leader. A smaller or under developed thumb shows less or not fully developed brain.

The Mount of Venus is located at the base of the thumb.(See *Fig.9*). But the relationship between this mount and the thumb is not as other mounts have with their joining fingers.

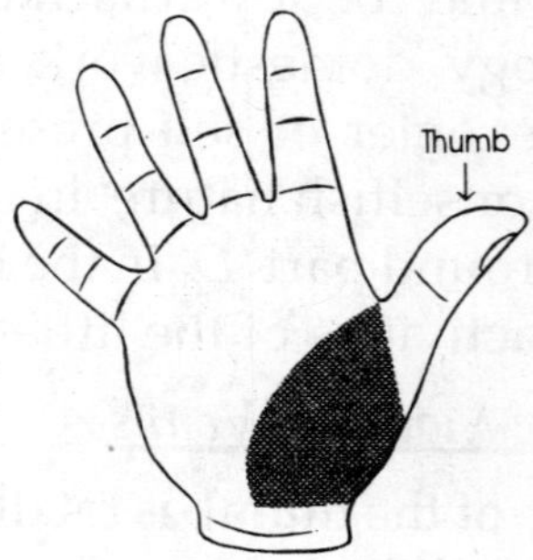

Fig. 9

Mount of Venus reveals one's vitality and his relationship with the fellow human beings which keeps on unveiling itself in the matter of love, affection, compassion, friendship and sex. Extra-developed Mount of Venus indicates overflow of vitality which often manifests itself in sexual relations. The physical attributes of Venus derive their strength through the Mercury and the little finger from the nervous system.

Nisha : Is it not strange that one vitality force reveals itself in compassion and friendship but it is also the source of sexual passions?

Answer : Nothing strange in it. It is one electric power which illuminates our house, heat our room and cool it also through the airconditioner. This because of the different appliances using the same power. The different centers in the brain inspire different harmonal secretions with the social bonds acting as different push buttons to activate the same power- current. That is why the different emotions are shown in different spheres – now in the affection for the progeny, now for the kith and kin, now in compassion and now in sex ! According to our hypothesis, its regulating center in the brain should be close to the center controlling the activities associated with Mount of Venus.

An underdeveloped Mount of Venus reflects dryness in the human relations. However, the presence of the semi circle small lines on this mount make it as potent as the developed one, A Mount of Venus without of lines indicates lack of emotion on the native's part. He may have no associate or he may not desire any association with anybody either. In the Fig.No. 4, the *E*-part is depicted related to the thumb and the *F*-part to the wrist region. Since the Mount of Venus is close to the wrist, the center controlling the emotions of love, compassion and sex must logically be located somewhere between or around E and F in the Fig.number 4.

The Mount of Moon or Luna

Just opposite to the Mount of Venus, the Luna Mount is located close to the wrist. Although no finger represents any attribute of this mount, the closest to it (position-wise) is the little finger which has a direct bearing upon the nervous systems. (See Fig.No. *10*)

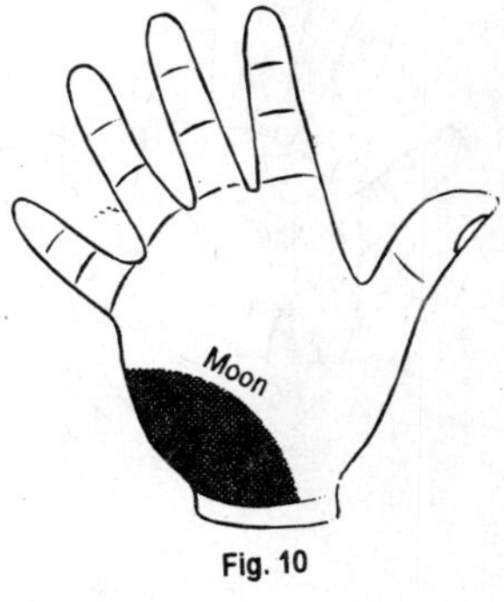

Fig. 10

Old palmists insist on the Moon having close relation with water, whose characteristic features are fickleness, mobility and instability. The same are said to be of the mind (*Munn*) also. However, being imaginative is also mind's another characteristic. Mixing all attributes together, we consider the Mount of Moon to be having a bearing upon the mind (*Munn*), its imaginative faculty and instability or amount representing journeys as well.

All the fine arts like music, poetry, painting etc. need the judicious blend of flight of imagination with a creative mind. Hence the other conducive symptoms on the hand, with a good Mount of Moon, make one a good artist. But the association of the inauspicious symptoms make one a psychic case and a day dreamer.

The line going from the Mount of Moon to the Mount of Mercury is called the line of intuition (See Fig.No. 11). Now, the intuitive power becomes possible only with the developed mind. This strengthens our hypothesis that the Mount of Moon indicates about one's power of imagination as also its measure.

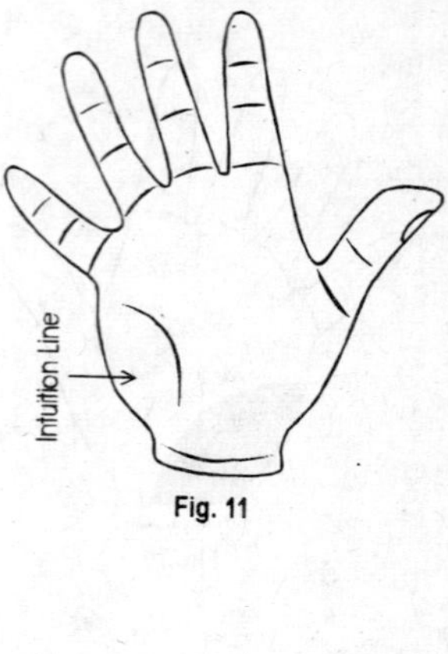

Fig. 11

Both ancient sages and the modern psychologists had and have always been trying to identify the place of the *Munn* inside the body. In case we are able to determine the center in the brain controlling the Mount of Moon we should deem as though we have succeeded in identifying the position of the mind (*Munn*) in the body.

This center may possibly be closer to the center controlling the wrist and the little finger which is depicted around or between *'D'* and *'F'* parts shown in the Fig.no. 4.

<u>*The Three Centers of Mars*</u>

Mars' characteristic traits are forbearance, bravery and courage. In palmistry Mars' big region is divided in three parts. The one between the Mounts of Jupiter and Venus is reckoned by old palmists as the 'lower Mars'. (See *Fig.No. 12*, the *'A'* part). The one between Mercury and Moon is 'upper Mars' (See *Fig.12* at *'B'*) and the middle part of the palm 'the plane of Mars' (See *Fig.12* at *'C'*).

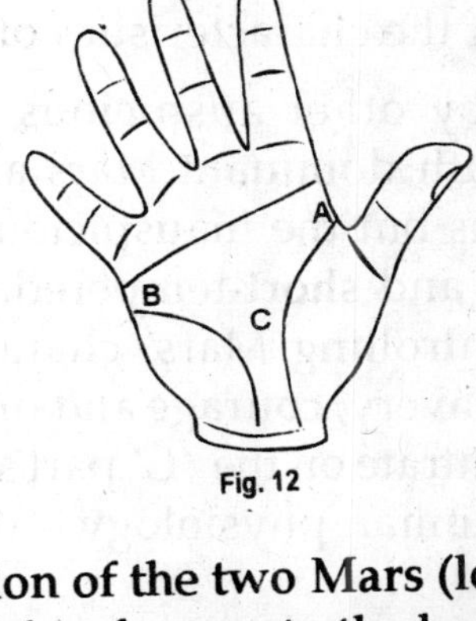

Fig. 12

The position of the two Mars (lower and upper) is determined with reference to the head line. But since the head line is not uniformly placed in every hand, we have rejected this style of reckoning in our books written earlier and given them different names. The one between the Mounts of Venus and Jupiter is named 'Aggressive Mars'. The argument is that since this is like an extention of the Mount of Venus and Venus is generally hot-tempered, this kind of Mars should indicate the dominating and, the wrath-related, qualities of this Martial Planet. It also reveals about the person's physical strength. Moreover, since, physical power is normally associated with bravery, the nomenclature : "Aggressive Mars" appears fully justified.

The other Mars located between the Mounts of Mercury and Moon (*Fig.12* at '*B*') is named 'Defensive Mars' by us. It is because the both mounts, that of Mercury and of Moon, have a close relation with nervous systems or the brain. Both planets have cool temperament. This coolness never makes an assault, it only forbears an aggression but refuses to accept defeat.

The middle part of the palm contains little extended parts of all the mounts (See *Fig.12* at '*C*') . If this portion appears developed, it is known as a heavy palm. A man with heavy palm is never despondent which is one of the characteristics of Mars as well.

Aided by other auspicious symptoms on the palm, those with dominant Mars are generally brave and courageous but the inauspicious symptoms make them arrogant and short-tempered. In order to locate the centers controlling Mars' characteristic traits like forbearance, bravery, courage and domineering nature, we must concentrate on the '*G*' part shown in the *Fig.no. 4* because in human physiology – this slot is reserved for the palm.

Nisha : You have pointed out a way for further research by studying the controlling centers in the brain of the fingers and the palm. At present it is only a hypothesis or a mere guessing, as to who will do this research and when?

Answer : True that this kind of research may be conducted only by a big team having psychiatrists, psychologists, experts from the medical field as also physio-philosophers working in total tandem with a well equipped laboratory needing billions of rupees. Although in near future there is no hope of getting such a team constituted, nevertheless, the institutions that spend millions of dollars for having the clone of a sheep; for getting a piece from the Moon-rocks and the sample of its soil will have to come one day to the forefront to identify these controlling centers in the human brain. This can happen with in or beyond my life time but I am hopeful.

Chapter III

HOW THE LINES ON THE PALM ARE FORMED

<u>Nisha</u> : You call the lines on the palm as the scrawling inscriptions of the unconscious mind and also maintain that for these inscriptions the unconscious mind uses the brain as its instrument. Will you please elaborate on it ?

<u>Answer</u> : Before presenting our hypothesis on the formation of the lines we present the hypothesis of yet another palmist while referring to some accepted facts.

In his book 'The Laws of Scientific Hand Reading' Benham writes that around us is spread an omnipotent material. Some call it the Buddha and some the electric current or God or the effect of many planets and heavenly bodies.[1]

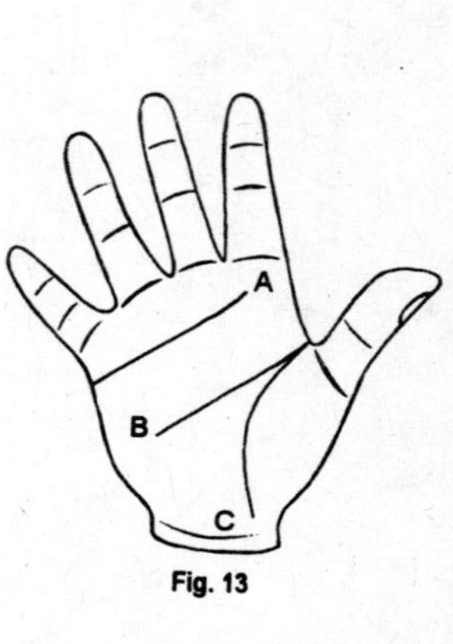

Fig. 13

In a chapter ahead Benham claims . that the life-current enters the body through the index fingers which first goes to form the Heart Line, (See *Fig.No. 13* at '*A*' thereafter, the Head Line (See *Fig.No. 13* at '*B*') and finally the Line of Life (See *Fig.No. 13* at '*C*').[2]

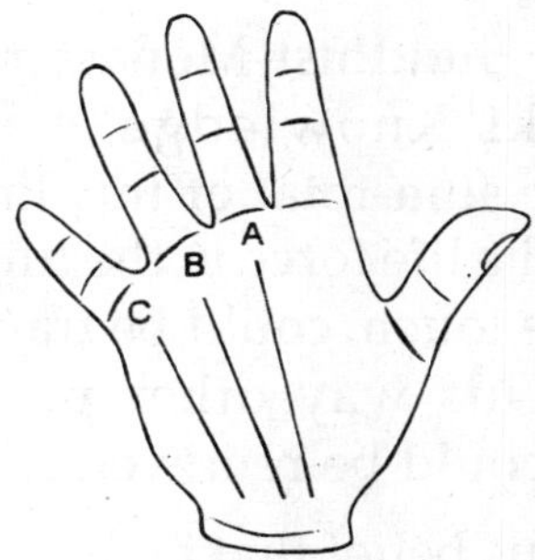

Fig. 14

In its return journey that life current forms first the Saturn-Line (*Fig.No. 14* at '*A*') and then the Sun-Line (*Fig.No. 14* at '*B*') and finally the Mercury-Line (*Fig.No. 14* at '*C*').[3]

Benham's this hypothesis gives the impression as though the life-current cycle is confined to the palm only. Benham claims that the entry of the life current takes place at the embryonic stage only.

According to Indian Scriptures the cause of life is deemed to be the conscious element which the Hindu seers call the soul. They deem the body to be a matter containing the mixture of the five basic elements which are the sky, air, fire, water and the earth. The entry of the soul into the five elements becomes the cause of life. However which path the soul adopts to enter the matter called the body has been a topic of long debate among the philosophers.

But instead of joining the debate we herewith mention about the other accepted facts.

According to Islamic concept, the heavenly beings predominant with the five elements called the *'Jinnaat'* enter the body through the nails of the fingers. It is these *'Jinnaat'* that make the person achieve miraculous feats.

It is in the Buddhist Monasteries in Tibet and Japan that 'Reiki Knowledge' had received its development. The sum-total of this knowledge is that by concentrating the life force in the fingers of the hand, this force, by mere touch, could be transmitted to other people's body. This way other people's causes of affliction or pain could be removed.

It is a famous belief that by the mere touch of his fingers Jesus, the Messiah, could remove other persons pain, distress and the disease.

The modern physiology and psychology assert that the whole of the human body is regulated by the nervous system placed in the brain. Often the brain is likened to an electric power station; with the nerves likened to the electric wires spread in the entire body and through them the brain regulates the entire body.

Also, the Chinese acu-puncture and acu-pressure therapies have identified various nerve centers in the body by putting pressure or puncturing them, the centers are activated which control a particular disease. In acu-pressure technique, however, such nerve-centers quite density exist on the palm.

Amidst these diverse and different opinions we want to remind you about the Somatosensory Area which reveals that the brain has deeper relations with the palm in comparison to its relations with the other body limbs. All these links have a definite bearing upon the formation of the lines on the palm.

Nisha : What kind of bearing ?

Answer : My intuition says that our nerves carry the electric current formed inside the brain. The mounts on our palm have a magnetic quality with every one of them attracting the electric current towards it that relates to the center of the brain is concerned with. These currents remain invisible till they reach the wrist. But as they enter the palm region from the wrist they reveal their path. With the result, the path of the movement of the electric-current becomes manifest. So, the lines on the hand show the path of there electric currents related to the particular mounts. The irregular path of this electric current's move is revealed in the shallow form or the broken lines.

Nisha : Your statement seems to tend towards one conclusion that the lines are not themselves the electric current but they show only its path. The second is, you seem to disagree with Benham's that life current enters the body through the index finger from outside and then it forms the three main lines; the Heart, the Head and the Life Lines It is in its return journey that it forms the secondary lines like the Saturn Line, the Sun Line and the Mercury Line.

Benham, however, is silent on the subsequent journey of the life-force. But you believe that the cause behind the formation of the three main lines is the unconscious mind and also assert that the mounts on the palm play a definite role in attracting the electric current issuing from the brain. You also claim that these electric currents remain invisible in their travelling the path upto the wrist after which they become manifest in the form of the lines. This belief, nevertheless, springs many questions. For instance some lines are slanted or horizontal; some are vertical

while some are circular. Some even cut each other to form a cross or a star. Some starts not from the base of the palm but from the middle of the palm. But where are the ways through which the electric current travels before it reaches the palm from the wrist? And why these are unmanifest till the current reaches the palm. Your hypothesis seems to be raising a plethora of questions, isn't it ?

Answer : All these questions had also sprung in my mind years before and since then I have been trying to search their answers. Now I shall reveal all of them which my study and research on this subject essay. But, first of all I tackle the question of invisibility of the electric-current's path till its reaching the end of the wrist. One related question was also mentioned by Benham in his book that when liver and the stomach are so far away from the tongue how the physician reveal their condition by examining the tongue.

In the same context I ask one question from you as well. How the doctors count the beat of the heart by counting the pulse rate. Surely the wrist (at which the pulse is felt) is much far from the heart ?

Nisha : **The veins and arteries transmitting the blood in the entire body from the heart spread to every extremity of the body. Since at the wrist these veins etc. are very close to the skin, the pulse rate counted there on gives much detail about the heart beat.**

Answer : Present in your this answer is also the answer to your question related to the formation of the lines on the palm. From the brain the nerves spread the electric current to every part of the body but these nerve-capillaries lie very close to the skin in the palm area. So the electric current that remains un-manifest, owing to the depth of the other parts of the body it is passing through, becomes manifest and visible as it reaches the palm.

The medical science had established a link between the tongue and the stomach, or between the pulse and the heart-beat through close examination. Later on with experiment, these links were established as facts. Palmistry, at present, is passing through that kind of the examination phase only and the establishments of such facts have yet to take place in certain cases. We have only put forth a hypothesis which may become a basis for further research and examination in this field.

Even Benham's hypothesis related to the life force is yet to be established but he had also indicated toward a definite direction. The arguments and counter arguments that have taken place regarding it, are being given here in the gist form. According to Benham's hypothesis, the life-force remains spread out of our body in the atmosphere which through the index finger enters the human body in its embryonic stage, although I don't agree with it.

Nisha : Then, when and how the main lines emerge on the palm of the child inside the womb ?

Answer : The basic effect of the main lines the infant inherit from his parents' genes. Out of these three the most essential line is that which we call the life line. It is present in every hand. However, the line of heart may remain absent in two percent persons and the line of head in almost one percent. Nevertheless, these two or three lines emerge when the child comes into the womb Almost its timing of manifestation Dr. Eugene Scheimann writes in his book : 'A Doctor's Guide to Better Health Through Palmistry' that the lines appear when the embryo is about three or four month old.

What I have to add to Dr. Scheimann's observation is this that the way the infant's anus, penis or vagina etc. remain inactive in that embryonic stage, the same way the ways to the transmission of the electric current remain dormant. The embrigo never pass the urine or stool inside the mother's womb but do so when they are delivered of. It is with the child's first cry that all his parts become functional. The ways of the movement of the electric current that a child inherits from his parent's gene become active immediately after the birth of the child.

According to Benham's hypothesis the life-force enters the human body through the index finger. I also want to add a bit to this hypothesis with an altered opinion that since our palm's part between the index finger and the thumb represent our basic instincts and the part of the palm between our little finger and the Mount of Luna represents our nerve system, that part concerns with our acquired traits .

<u>Nisha</u> : Please elaborate in details about the basic, natural and acquired traits or instincts.

<u>Answer</u> : Our basic instincts are : fear, anger, sleep, hunger, thirst, sex and self-preservation or the retention of our identity. These are called basic because no body teaches them but these are the instincts that a child is born with, and he reveal himself at due time. These are also called the natural instincts. They are common between man and animal.

<u>Nisha</u> : You reckon retention of one's identity as one of the basic instincts. It means insisting on one's recognition as the distinct entity. But to my mind this should be an acquired instinct represented by the Mount of Jupiter which makes us maintain one's individuality.

Answer : As soon as a child comes to his or her senses it wants to have complete monopoly over the mother's lap. This tendency to have monopoly is another form of one's retaining one's identity. Even in the tamed dog this tendency of possessiveness is apparent. It won't let his foster-master's affection be shared by anybody else. The moment a dog sees another entering its exclusive domain, it would like to shoo it away by incessant barking.

On the contrary, the sense of brotherhood is our acquired trait which makes man social. Even a child learns it while getting the opportunity. Animals also develop it. We learn it in accordance with our scale of profit and loss. The desire to earn fame or be identifiable even in a crowd is the developed form of that trait; to retain one's identity. Of course the desire of leadership is also its culminated form only which is the characteristic of the well developed Mount of Jupiter.

The part below this mount which we call Aggressive Mars is the extention of the Mount of Jupiter and Venus.

The Mount of Venus represents our that body made of flesh and bones which we have inherited from our ancestors and which we have to bequeath to our descendents. It is the mount of the vitality whose over flow subsequently shows in the form of sexual feelings or libido.

This vital power also shows in our anger when we dislike something. A man also becomes angry when his ego is hurt. Hence our calling the Aggressive Mars as the extention of the Mounts of Jupiter and Venus.

One's exploding in anger is tantamount to bursting of a volcano with the lava flowing out. In case this is suppressed the anger manifest in the form of jealousy leading to various tensions and depressions. This change of form of expression is caused by lack of vitality power vis-a-vis the well developed nervous systems. The Mount of Mercury and the Moon represent the nervous system on the palm.

However, when jealousy gets coupled with other distinctive instincts it may lead to hatching of conspiracies and intrigues. If the Mount of Moon be commanding strong attraction then the anger changes its form to appear in the expression of satire, poetry, music, painting etc; or in the various other manifestation of the fine arts.

It is the coolness of the Moon, heat in Mars, the prudence and adjustibility of Mercury according to the situation that make the person forbearing and tolerant. He doesn't attack but by his cool patience and forbearance he fails the attack. This is the typical characteristic of the Defensive Mars. That is why, according to our belief, the Defensive Mars (Mount) is the extention of the Mounts of Mercury and of the Moon.

An undeveloped Defensive Mars makes one lose one's patience and become a patient of tension and depression. It there be other adverse symptoms the man with undeveloped Defensive Mars may turn mad or even commit suicide.

Nisha : You seem to have resolved many riddles of psychology. No doubt this elaboration is quite enlightening but I am still to get answer to my question; how the lines are formed and how the various signs like cross, island, star etc. get formed on the palm.

If according to your hypothesis all lines on the palm are the ways the electric current issuing from

various centers of the brain pass through, all the lines should be vertical going from the wrist to the fingers. But some of them become slanted or even horizontal while some vanish in the middle of the palm without reaching near any mount at all. What are the reasons behind this phenomenon ?

Answer : My elaboration thus far is an introduction to my answer to this query. Since many varied subjects' study has helped me develop this sympothesis it is not out of place to give a brief background of the same. However, in order to answer the question relating to the formation of the various signs and criss-crossing, slanting and horizontal lines, I will have to divide the entire palm into many sections while adding a bit more fresh information also.

While introducing to the brain centers we told that the mounts on the palm have a magnet like quality. Add to this information that some part of the palm also possess the insulating qualities which check the flow of the electric current.

But it is only the weak currents that get checked; the stronger ones wind their way in a slanting or horizontal, even in askew manner to reach the concerned mount from the particular brain center. Some get blocked and form a kind of an island around the insulating parts of the palm. These insulators could also be near or far from the wrist and even in the middle of it. The electric currents remain invisible in the insulating part and re-emerge after the insulation is covered. (See *Fig.15,* a hand full of obstacles).

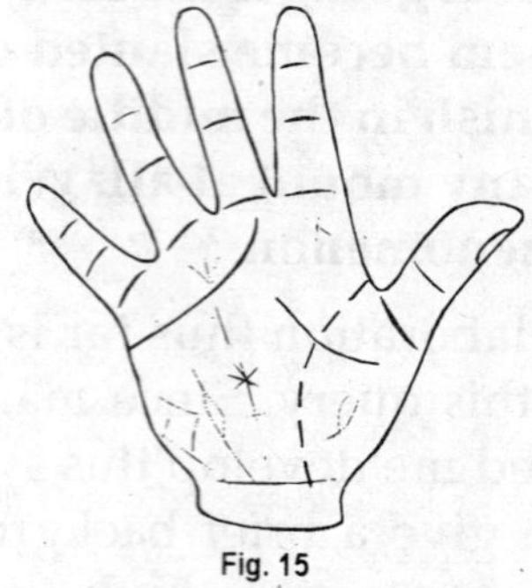

Fig. 15

Before understanding the cause behind the formation of the star, cross, a fish sign, trident etc. keep in the mind that the position of the Mount of Venus is different from the other mounts on the palm. Hence those lines attracted by the Venus Mount may get a bit slanted to go towards the mount or to the thumb.

It should also be kept in the mind that the space acquired by the mount of Venus is much more than that acquired by other mounts on the base of the fingers. Although the Mount of Luna (Moon) may have equal space on the palm as the Venus has, the Moon (Luna) Mount has no finger of its own. That is why the lines getting drawn to these two opposite mounts and originating from either the thumb or the little finger may form the signs when they encounter the lines going towards the other mounts. These signs have been named by the earlier palmists in accordance with the known figures or the mathematical signs. For instance, fish, trident, cross, star etc. .

Hence I would like to remind that it is our three main lines that we inherit from our ancestor's genes which are further nourished by our unconscious mind. There are the branches of these main lines that go to form the other lines. Subjected to various pulls or pushes of the other lines (carrying the electric-current or life-force). They form a variety of figures, give or seize power to and from other supporting lines. This causes the origin of the Line of Life near or adjoining with the head line.(See *Fig.16*). Very rare hands are those that have some distance between the life and head lines. (See Fig.*No. 17*). This may be due to the presence of the insulator in between. In most of the cases the line of life and the line of head have almost this common point of origin.

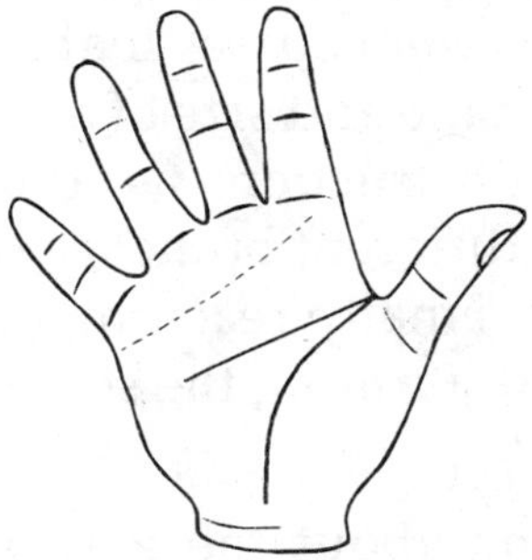

Fig. 16

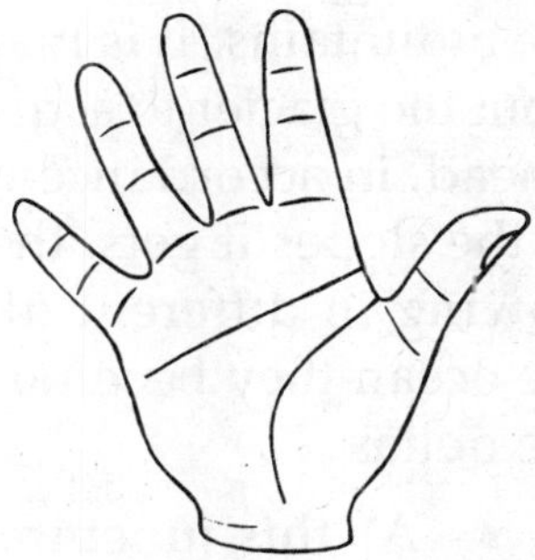

Fig. 17

The line of life moves in a semi-circular way towards the wrist. If there be an insulator it stops before reaching the wrist. (See *Fig.No. 18*). Else, its reaching the wrist-point, it may start its transaction with the electric currents sent by the brain center which provide it due energy. These electric currents coming from the brain centers get augmented by the energy or inspiration received from the unconscious mind which makes them much more powerful. If the Head Line and Life Line may have started from the common point the energy thus doubled of the Life Line also makes the Head Line even stronger.

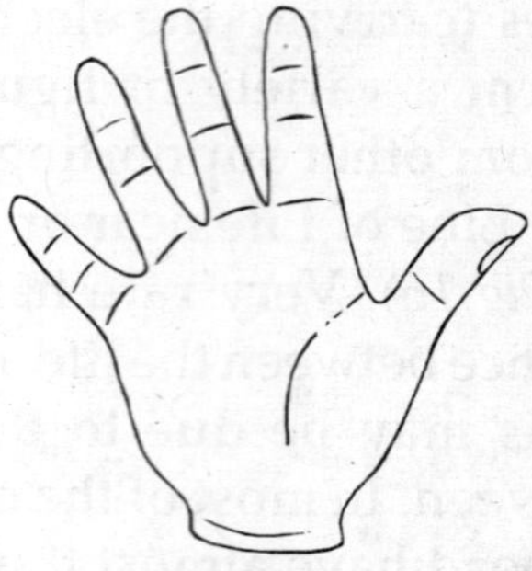

Fig. 18

I would like to clarify my this point by drawing an analogy from the rivers issuing from the glacier in the mountains. It is many tiny water courses that issue from the glacier to acquire the shape and size of a river. Ahead, in accordance with the obstructions faced by it or the slopes it gets, the river's different branches start flowing in different directions. Finally reaching close the ocean they become scattered, forming the scores of the deltas.

At this juncture referring about the nature of lakes, springs and step-wells is also necessary.

Although apparently then springs, lakes, step-wells or wells appear to have no connection with any mountain or river, yet the fact is that every water source has some connection either with any river or mountain or rain-fall, glacier or a volcano. During our travels, we saw hot and cool springs existing very close to each other. The curious fact is that the hot springs are as hot as to boil rice when dropped in them while the cool springs as cold as the melted ice. Obviously their sources must be hundreds of miles apart from each other. But the springs with totally different water temperatures do exist close to each other. Coming from the far-off sources the subterranean streams wind their way on different routes due to the presence of the obstructions on their way. But as soon as the obstructions get removed they emerge like the springs. A cluster of such springs get the identity in the form of some lake or the step-well.

This evident fact of geography I want to mention while explaining my hypothesis in palmistry concerning the electric currents emerging from various brain center. These currents, the insulators, the power transmitted by the unconscious mind, the magnetic power of the palm – all collectively cause the lines on the hand. Some of them tread their full course while some vanish in the middle.

This way the theory propounded by us regarding the formation of the two of the three main lines – the lines of Life and Head – and other secondary lines stands explained and duly presented by us. However, in understanding the cause behind the formation of the third main line – the Heart Line – we did encounter some difficulty. It is because neither it is joined like the Head and the Life Lines nor there is any apparent way of its creation from the electric currents issuing from the different brain centers (See *Fig. No. 19*). Starting from or nearby the Mount of Jupiter it reaches close to the Defensive Mars. I declare its origin to be the unconscious mind.

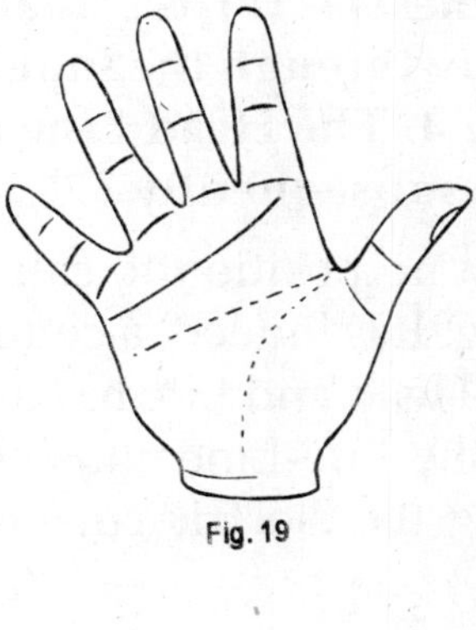

Fig. 19

However, Benham gives maximum importance to the Line of Heart. Keeping this fact in view, we remind the readers about the Islamic belief that the Supernatural Being with predominance of the element of fire, also called *'Jinnaat'*, enter the body through the medium of the nails on the finger. Benham's theory is that it is the index finger through which the life-current, spreading outside, enters the body. According to the Indian *Saamudrik Shashtra* (The Science of revealing one's life through the study of one's various limbs) the area in which the Mount of Venus is located is our *'Gotra'*s origin. Loosely *Gotra* means the lineage of the community we belong to. This fact must also be borne in mind that nearest to this mount is our thumb which in palmistrical lexicon gets more importance than the fingers.

It appears as through all these diverse beliefs and concepts have a relationship but the joining links are missing. Nevertheless, these facts do indicate that apart from the unconscious mind there are certain powers which enter our body from outside and reach upto our brain. Or it is quite possible that following their collision with the insulation they might be changing their course as well.

Nisha : Should it be taken from this explanation that Benham's hypothesis is correct ; that outside life-force entering the body through the index finger forms the Line of Heart first. The Head Line and the Life Line are formed by it subsequently ?

Answer : I am in no position to call any hypothesis to be right or wrong. It is indeed, a common occurrence to find the Lines of Head and Life having a common point of origin. Since the Life-Line ends close to the wrist it may be receiving the electric current issued from the relevant brain center. And through the medium of this line the Head Line may also be getting the electric current (See *Fig. No. 20*). But they appear to have no connection with the Line of Heart. However, there ought to be an insulator in between because it is deemed auspicious to have some distance between the Head Line and the Heart Line.

In such a situation the Heart Line inherited by the genes is left with one source of energy; that it receives energy from the unconscious mind. I am still to think over the various links that may give a clue to this line's (Heart Line's) getting additional energy.

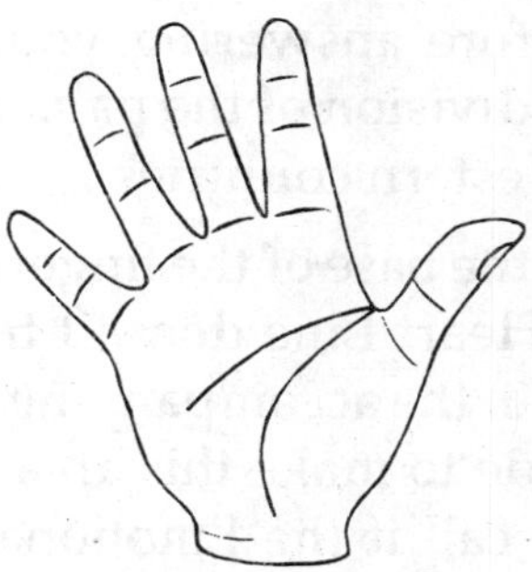

Fig. 20

<u>Nisha</u> : You are yourself admitting that these missing links have still to be revealed by your hypothesis. We shall wait eagerly for that research. However, there are some questions that still spring up, related to the horizontal lines on the Mount of Mercury which the western palmists call Lines of Marriage (see *Fig. No. 21* at *'A'*); the horizontal lines on the Mount of Venus and the Aggressive Mars which are normally called the worry lines (See *Fig. No. 21* at *'B'*); the horizontal and vertical lines on the Mount of Luna (See *Fig. No. 21* at *'C'* and *'D'*) which are called the journey lines.

The same way there are other lines including the girdle of Venus etc. How these lines are formed ?

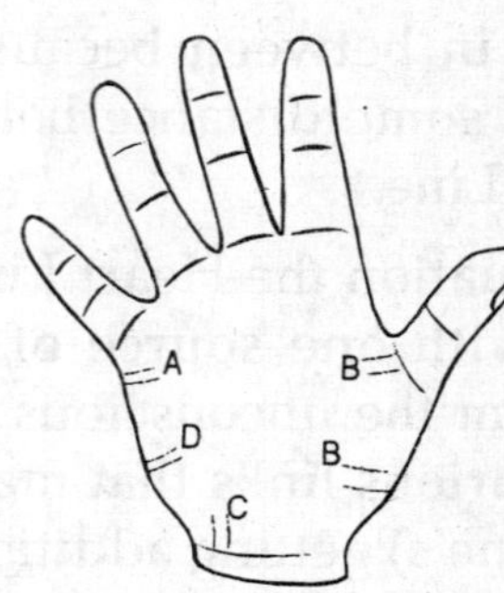

Fig. 21

Answer : But before answering your this question I must tell you the division of the palm suggested by the palmists of the Western countries.

Division – 1 From the base of the fingers upto the Line of Heart. Since the Heart Line doesn't travel straight but in a circular way, in the accompanying figure the dotted line has been made to make this area rectangular. The western palmists call it the Emotional Area (See *Fig. No.* 22 at '*A*')

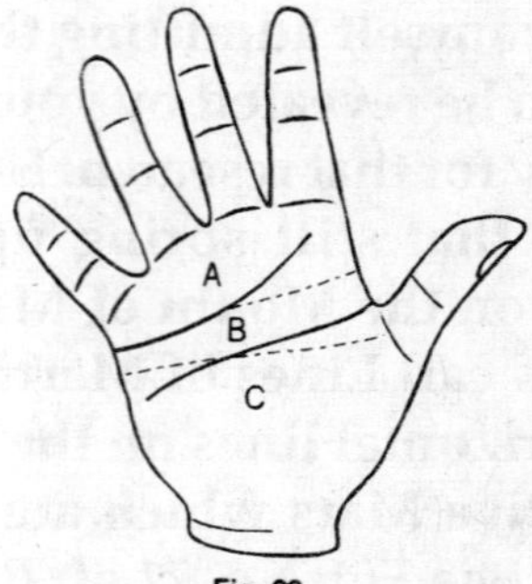

Fig. 22

<u>*Division – 2*</u> From the lower border of the Emotional Area upto the Head Line (The dotted line) called the Practical Area (See *Fig. No. 22* at '*B*').

<u>*Division – 3*</u> From the Practical Area to the wrist (See *Fig. No. 22* at '*C*') is called the Physical Area. This relates to the person's basic instincts.

These divisions made by the western palmists have been found to be quite logical by me to a great extent. But it is still not the final truth.

Now, besides these three horizontal divisions we also give three vertical areas divided in accordance with our hypothesis. That division is made the following way. (See *Fig. No. 23*)

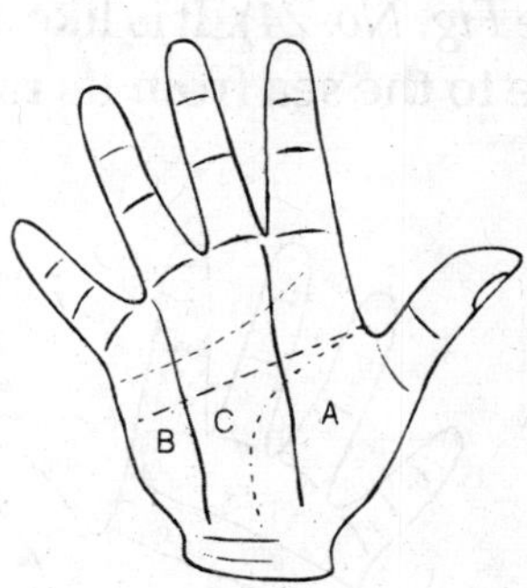

Fig. 23

1. The area between the thumb and the index finger represents the human body's muscle - bone and flesh part (See *Fig. No. 23 A*). All the basic instincts that a man inherits from his ancestors are represented by this part on the palm. Thus, according to our hypothesis, it is the place of origin of the three main lines.

2. The vertical area between the little finger and the Mount of Moon which represents the nervous system (See *Fig. No. 23* at '*B*'). This area also relates to a person's mental development.

3. The vertical area between the other two vertical areas bound by the Mounts of Sun and Saturn above and the wrist below (See *Fig. No.* 23 at 'C'). This has the characteristics of the Mounts of Jupiter and Mercury intermingled. Moreover, this area is the joining area between the two other areas. The wordliwiseness of Mercury conjoins with Sun's extrovertness to create the longing in the nature for renown and fame. The Jupiter Mount's insistence on maintaining the identity is balanced by the effect from the Mount of Saturn.

Now, if the two divisions – the one by the western palmists and the other derived by us – are studded together, the conclusion is that the journey of the Heart and the Head Lines is from the basic to the acquired tendencies (See *Fig. No.* 24). It is like a river flowing down the slopy plane to the sea from its raised point of origin.

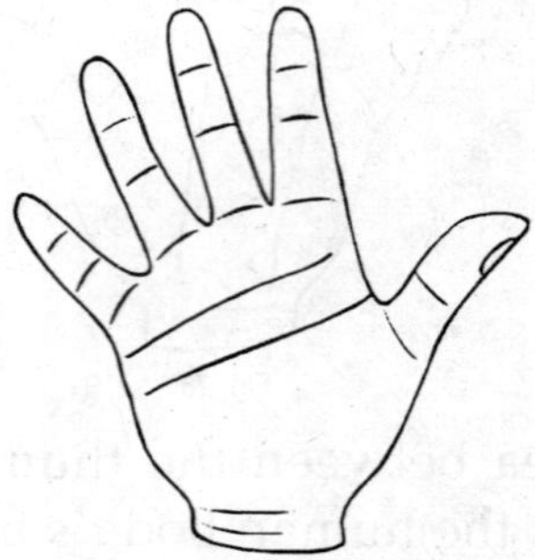

Fig. 24

Some hands have the Heart Line quite close to the fingers (See *Fig. No.* 25), while some have the Heart Line close to the Head Line (See *Fig. No.* 26). This proves that in the hands which have the Emotional Area attracted by the surrounding four mounts have the Heart Line close to the fingers. However, those that have the domineering attraction for the practical area have the Heart Line sliding closer to the line of Head.

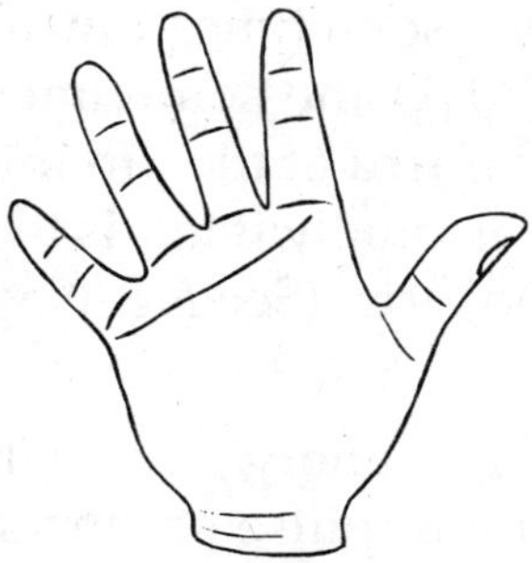
Fig. 25

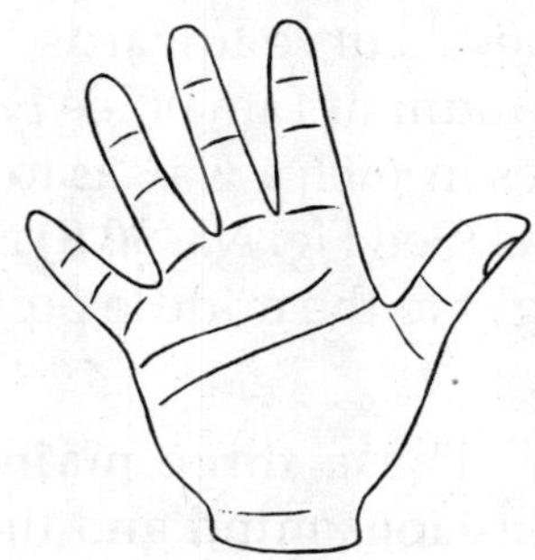
Fig. 26

The mounts also contribute in regulating the direction of both these lines When the attraction be more towards the Mount of Mercury, these lines get drawn toward this Mount (See *Fig. No.27*) similarly the greater attention towards the Mount of Luna tilts these lines towards this mount. (See *Fig. No. 28*). In case the two mounts' attraction be even, these lines tend to go toward the Defensive Mars (See *Fig. No. 29*).

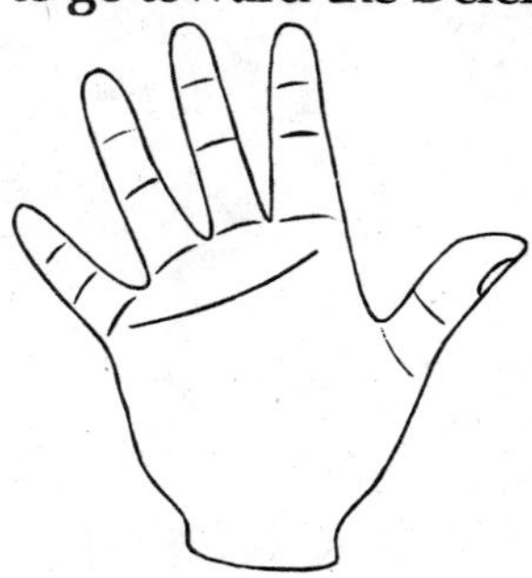
Fig. 27

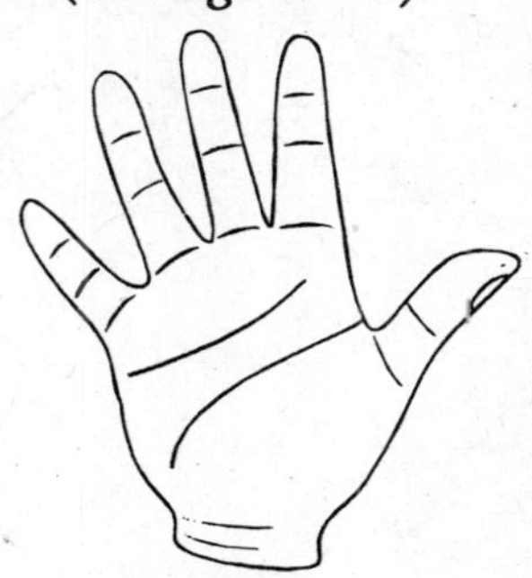
Fig. 28

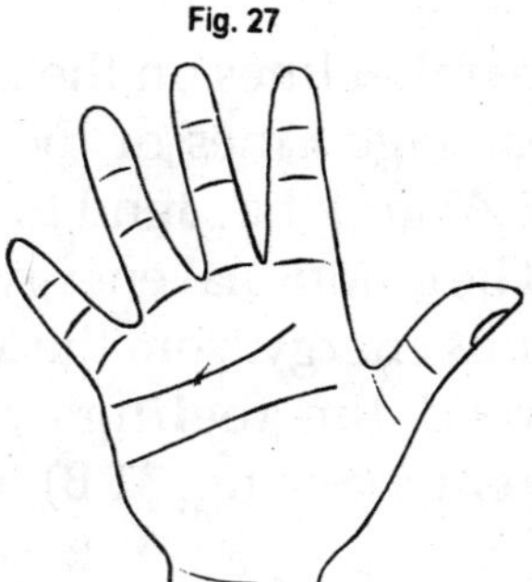
Fig. 29

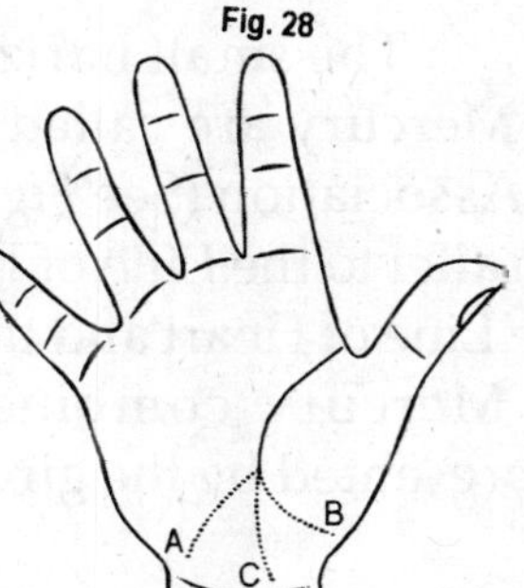

Fig. 30

The Life Line's initial part emerges below the Mount of Jupiter. There after, below the Saturn Mount it takes a curve towards the wrist, sometimes towards the Mount of Luna (See *Fig. No. 30 A*) and sometimes it moves in such a way as to limit the area of the Mount of Venus (See *Fig. No. 30 B*) and occasionally it tends to go straight to the middle point of the wrist (See *Fig. No. 30 C*).

These three main lines get energy from the unconscious mind and the electric impulse or currents emerging from the brain centers which cause them burst out in the branch lines or the parallel lines. Then parallel lines are like those springs which have their sources far off but which appear close the moment the obstructions among them get removed.

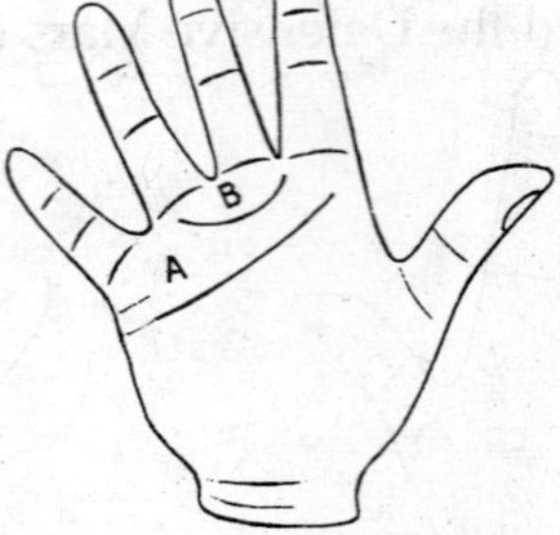

Fig. 31

The small horizontal parallel lines on the Mount of Mercury are called the Marriage Lines or the Lines of Association (See *Fig. No. 31 A*) and they tend to travel parallel to the Line of Heart. The emotional energy from the Line of Heart and the nervous energy from the Mount of Mercury combine to breed the feelings of sex represented by the girdle of Venus (See fig. 31 B), which is also a parallel line to the Heart Line. Of course that girdle has no direct contact with the Venus Mount but the attractions from the Mount of Sun (also called Apollo) and the Mount of Saturn intermingle with the emotional aspect of the Heart Line to make the native extremely emotional. Hence in my opinion the presence of the girdle of Venus on the hand make the native more emotional but not more sexy.

As far as your question : as to why don't' all the lines tend to go towards the direction of the fingers, its answer is somewhat long which is given ahead.

The Head Line and the Life Line are the lines closest to the position of the thumb. Since the area of the Venus Mount is rather large, it is natural for it to have more magnet-like attraction. But, as is apparent, its direction is opposite to the placement of the mounts on the base of the fingers.

However, the area covered by the Mount of Luna is rather as big as that of the Mount of Venus. So logically the Mount of Moon must also have greater attraction. As told, the length of the Head Line, the Life Line and the bigger area of the Mount of Moon may explain the causes behind some lines being a bit slanted or even horizontal. It is on account of their area of effectiveness that they are named accordingly – like the Venus' Mount representing the family area. There the criss-cross of the lines represent the familial worries while the Mount of Moon represents the fickleness or changeability of the mind. But the criss-cross of the lines there is said to be the plethora of the journey lines, although their full consequence is revealed by studying other lines and symptoms on the hand as well.

The fact is that our hypothesis indicates towards one direction. Doing research and further study in that particular direction may lead us to a definite result.

Nisha : Your conclusions are the end result of your painstaking study of the various subjects, disciplines and practices which include the spiritual knowledge, psychology, philosophy as well as the medical science. It is only he is capable of giving his opinion on your conclusions or hypothesis who himself has covered all these diverse subjects in his study.

At the moment, my query is : could these be a measure or method which may turn the electric currents or impulses favourable or unfavourable at will? Or, can a person's basic nature be altered by any means ?

Answer : To a certain extent their effect can be accentuated or lessened. Else there may not be any usefulness of this knowledge. These measures are called the remedies upon whose scientific-orientation we shall be throwing light in the coming pages.

References

1, 2, 3 Benham, William G; The Laws of Scientific Hand Reading; Mumbai, D.B., Taraporevala Sons & Co, (1975), p. 354 to 356.

Chapter IV

THE LOGIC BEHIND THE REMEDIES TO REMOVE OBSTACLES

No one comes to the physician for knowing what disease he is suffering from but for learning about it so that one could also learn about its possible remedy.

Similarly any one coming to show his hand to the palmist comes with the objective of knowing about the cause of his affliction in order to have it cured. Hence it is necessary for a good palmist to have a fair knowledge about the remedy for the adverse symptoms or lines found present in the client's hand.

Nisha : Is it necessary that only aggrieved or afflicted persons may come to the palmist ? After all, there could also be persons curious about knowing this science and about their future.

Answer : Of course, curiosity can also drive them to Palmist. But in general, more than 90% persons come to the palmist when they are afflicted with some trouble. However, their troubles are, in general, more psychological or mental than physical. Some might be needing money and wealth, some may come for getting a good job. Love problems, matrimonial unhappiness etc. are the other reasons behind the person seeking a counselling from the palmists. Some might be worried about their son's future, some might be seeking quick riddance from the debt-load. Also come to the palmists some very ambitious persons; they are not satisfied with what they possess, they hanker after more and more. When they fail to do so, they get puzzled and seek the palmist's guidance.

Nisha : Will the remedial measures give employment to the unemployed? Will the love-lorn beloved and lover get bound in the nuptial bound? Will a debtor get respite from his creditors? Will the parents unable to arrange required dowry for their nubile daughter get the needed sum or will they succeed in getting the marriage solemnised without the need for the dowry? Will the divorce seeking couple get the divorce by these remedial measures suggested by a palmist ?

Answer : It is not possible to say 'yes' to all your questions so easily. However, quoting an example from the other field I would try to give answer to your queries.

You know that the business of the insurance companies is quite thriving. These insurance companies insure people for life. There is another kind of medical insurance to cover various expenses. There are insurance schemes to cover various accidents caused by fire, earth quake, riots and other similar damages. People get insured when they undertake journey in road-travel, air-travel and sea-travel They have transit insurance for the goods. There are insurance schemes to cover even dacoity, theft etc. These insurance companies, against a nominal premium assure us that in the event something untoward happening they will compensate us. The good companies, in fact, fulfil their commitment as well.

These insurance companies give commission to their agents and salary to their staff. Apart from maintaining the façade of flamboyance in their office-building, installation etc. they give bonus also to the staff and to those booked under their insurance. But despite all these expenses, they earn good profit. Can you suggest why ?

Nisha : No, but I would like to know the reason.

Answer : It is this. The untoward happening or damage that we fear or apprehend is more feared than its actually taking place. We insure ourselves against that fear. This is the secret of the insurance companies' thriving business. The figures or statistics that these companies have, indicate that there are actually much less number of persons who face the trouble against which they insure themselves. But those who gets insured are much more. With the result, these insurance companies get much more money from the premiums they regularly receive and in actual practice they have to pay much less compensation money. That is the reason of these insurance companies doing well financially. In general, they always earn profit.

Now, your question about the suggested remedial measures actually doing the needful. The answer is no! Only the remedial measures cannot do the needful. But till the time their problems are solved which may be due to other extraneous reasons, the apprehended persons would get a good moral support by the remedial measures to provide extra strength to them to face the odd situation. With fortified morale they would be able to fight well in the unpleasant situation.

These remedies which the palmist suggests to the afflicted persons include the incantations (*Mantra*) according to the person's belief. the *Taveeza, (yantras)* (Amulettes or *talisman*) advice on keeping fasts, donating alms, doing meditation, saying prayers, wearing a ring with a specific gem etc.

As I told you the purpose of these remedial measures is to boost the person's morale. This way they get considerable riddance from their phobia, fears etc. Some people always remain apprehensive, fearing the worst, with the result, they deprive themselves of the pleasures and comforts they could get even in the existing situation. These remedies take care of their phobias and they feel somewhat relieved from the apprehended adversity or misfortune. With the revival of hope they are spared from a variety of mental problems they would have succumbed to. These remedial measures can even detract them from the madness of committing suicide.

Normally, the problems in business and employment are invariably of short duration. Most of them get solved with the passage of time. With these remedial measures they get a kind of respite to pass their apprehended days.

In the cases related to love, divorce, marriage etc. there could be two final decisions; either favourable or unfavourable. Also, any decision favourable to the defendant is bound to be unfavourable to the plantiff. In short the possibility or the probability factor in such cases is 50 : 50. But the figure about those that get troubled by such problems is 100 percent. Following the remedial measures in accordance with one's faith they do derive a moral strength and protect themselves from the further aggravation of the trouble. Also, this relief from the apprehension would help them retain their composure with which they can think with an unperturbed mind. They can, then, hit upon the desired solution by their own prudence and achieve the needful. It is a psychological fact that hope and apprehension (fear) cannot occupy one's mind at the same time. Only one of them can exist at one time. With hope having 50% chances of its getting fulfilled the native gets the reassuring feeling of achieving one's desired goal at least half way already with these remedial measures.

The English idiom : 'time is a great healer' has been rephrased by *Mirza Ghalib* by saying : *"Dard Ka hada se guzarna hai davaa ho jana."* (Excessive pain itself emerges as its cure.). The meaning is clear. If a pain survives for long, it enhances one's capacity to suffer which in turn lessens the intensity of the pain.

For an unhappy person every moment appears full of grief. In these moments there remedies surge forth a wave of hope in the melancholic heart to lessen the weight of grief.

In fact the remedies' role comes afterwards. First of all, one's revealing the cause of one's grief before the palmist reduces the burden on his heart considerably. In a modern fast-paced world who has the time to listen to other's woes? In such a situation a sympathetic pair of ears before the aggrieved person works wonders for the afflicted.

I give all these details to impress you that it is this process itself which solves 70 percent of the problems for those who repose faith in the remedial measures, since they act as a soothing balm to the person bitterly in pain of his or her personal worries which are not revealable before all. We claim 70 percent success by personal experience which is surely more than the relevant data concerning the patient's cure by the physicians.

<u>Nisha</u> : It is rather presumptuous on your part to claim 70 percent success for those who repose faith in the remedial measures. How can you be so sure about it

and how can you claim this percentage is less for those that go to the physician for getting cured of their physical afflictious. Another corollary to this question which is obvious : What if that kind of faith in the remedial measures be absent ?

<u>Answer</u> : Lack of faith in the remedies can reduce the advantage to a big zero. Because without faith even the most seasoned doctors can not cure their patients. Whether it be a *Mantra* or a prayer, it is the faith in their efficacy that boost the person's morale. In case the remedy be wearing some gem in the ring, it acts two ways. First, the gem if worn in the right finger provides energy to the relevant Mount's brain center and thus helps to develop like the suppressed mount. Secondly, that gem in the ring will keep on reminding the person as to with what objective that has been worn. This is a kind of psychological treatment which enhances the efficacy of the gem.

<u>Nisha</u> : **Your hypothesis concerning the brain center's controlling the relevant mounts is based on your guessing only. Suppose your that guessing be rather baseless ?**

<u>Answer</u> : But having the specific gem embedded in a ring according to the *Rashi* (The moon sign in the horoscope) is an old practice. I have only tried to search the scientific reason behind this practice which is still in the conjectural form. But there is no denying the fact that the specified gem does cast the psychological effect upon the wearer. It keeps on remaining the purpose behind that person's wearing it.

It is an old saying in Hindi : "Tie it into a knot" (i.e. remember it always). It means tie a knot in your hanky or any other apparel that you have on your body so that by looking at the knot you may ever be reminded of that purpose. Even those with weak memory may also be reminded by looking at that knot. These gems embedded in a ring also serve this very purpose. Their constant view keeps on giving you a sort of mental injection to remember the objective of wearing them. This definitely keeps the person's morale high. We have conjectured that the specified gem does provide strength to the relevant brain center which is an additional advantage.

Furthermore, the claim made of 70 % success is supported by a very scientific theory of probability. It claims that in any venture a person has 50 percent chances of success and 50 % of failure. The 20% extra has been added owing to the faith that the person may have in the suggested remedial measures which surely boosts up morale. A good and timely advise can bring an entire change in the situation. Even any extraneous – say political – reason may also effect the desired change in the situation. You never know.

Your other question is : on what basis have we claimed that the figure of the medicine suggested by a physician may be less efficacious than these remedial measures. Before giving its answer I give an example of the dreadful disease called AIDS.

This term is derived from four words' first letters: Acquired Immune Deficiency Syndrome. It means the deficiency or failure of the system's inherent immunisation mechanism.

You know that thus for AIDS has no cure. It is fatal for the person afflicted by it. Why it is incurable? Because its viruses destroy the system's self's immunisation mechanism.

Normally, our body keep on fighting with the various germs or viruses. This immune system keeps destroying the viruses which if left undestroyed may cause various diseases. We are hardly aware of this battle being carried on inside our body and suddenly we feel we have become healthy again. Any concussion, blow, cold or other diseases are immediately taken care of by our defense mechanism . The physician's medicine reinforces only our this mechanism. But the battle is always won when our defense mechanism is strong.

In case this defense mechanism, is destroyed, no matter what medicine is administered the cure becomes impossible. In that situation even a minor ailment can prove fatal.

By giving this example my intention is to impress, that no matter how good be a physician or how effective, be the medicine the cure is achieved by our body's strong defense mechanism. Medicine only helps this mechanism. We would go to the extent of claiming that if the defense-mechanism is allowed full play even without any external medicine our body can get rid of any infection etc. But the reverse is not true. In this event, with our defense mechanism failing, no medicine can cure us. This way, perhaps, you can realise that it is more than the psychological impact of taking the medicine than the efficacy of it which proves more effective even in the case of the physician and the patient.

After all, medicine is just a matter while the body is also matter made of five elements. Matter can treat matter, but mind is not matter. So by providing additional strength to the mind a disease could be cured in a more effective manner. Faith acts like an anchor to the fickle mind to stabilise it. Like the sailors drop the anchor to stabilise their ship in a tempest, the same way these remedial measures like the gem in the ring, the fasts, the vows, the prayers, the *Mantra* etc. are used to keep the mind on an even keel.

Worry, fear, apprehension etc. are the afflictions of the mind which breed tension and depression to cast bad effect on the physical body as well. Of course the medicines are required to treat a sick physical body but unless the mind is also treated simultaneously, the medicines may not prove very efficacious. A well-wishing fortune teller suggests the remedial measures in accordance with the faith the native adheres to, for treating his mind as well.

Nisha : An astrologer may suggest the needed gem to the native by studying his horoscope. What is the basis for a palmist to suggest such measures ?

Answer : By studying the symptoms on the hand as revealed by the fingers and the mounts. If a finger or a mount be undeveloped the required gem should be suggested to make good the deficiency. In case the mounts be over-developed, their influence should also be lessened by suggesting the gems that may strength the mounts giving the counter influence.

Nisha : The mounts giving the counter influence ? Please make it clear.

Answer : I have given the scientific basis behind the remedial measures. I shall tell you about their practical aspects, ahead, at the due place.

Chapter V

THE POSSIBILITIES BEFORE THE SCIENTIFIC PALMISTRY

Nisha : Why do you insistently desire that Palmistry should be reckoned as a scientific knowledge. For centuries together it is deemed to be an occult science. What is the harm if it is continued to be reckoned that way only ?

Answer : Many big industrialists, tycoons and top political leaders keep consulting the palmists clandestinely but outwardly they always pretend their non-belief in these kind of occult sciences. In fact, it has become a fashion to privately believe in these but publicly denounce them as pure superstition. The result is this knowledge – palmistry – is not getting its due honour.

So, in case its scientific basis could be known, it might get as much honour as is given to psychology.

Psychology has many branches now : medical psychology, experimental psychology, social psychology and the like which are put to their relevant use in various industries and hospitals. According to one branch of it a person's physical age and his intellectual age is determined on the basis of the Intelligent Quotient or I Q. Even the law courts recognise it like a doctor's certificate.

Now psychology – the subject – has a machine invented to conduct the 'lie-detector test' and the efforts are on to have its conclusions accepted as evidence by the law courts.

Some medical experts and physicians in the US and Europe have attempted to identify the disease, Cancer, on the basis of the capillaries present on the person's palm. Normally this diagnosis would have required many tests involving lot of time and expenditure.

Some decades ago the diseases like epilepsy were deemed to be the afflictions created due to the person's possession by the ghostly spirits which were treated by the exorcists. But now they have been brought into the purview of psychological treatment. Now every good hospital has a psychiatry center where many psychiatrists work.

By my hypothesis I want to establish that palmistry is closer to psychology owing to its certain fundamentals which need to be further verified through clinical tests. But arranging those kinds of facilities and resourses are beyond a single - like me - person's capacity. Once this is taken as science, may be, many scientific institutions would come forward to have the needed research conducted with their resources. Consequently, many palmists will also get their due recognition and benefits.

Nisha : According to you, once this knowledge gets established as a scientific knowledge, it would automatically get recognition in the law courts, hospitals etc. Apart from this what do you visualise about scientific palmistry's scope in practical life?

Answer : It has scope in every walk of life. Following its establishment as the scientific knowledge, a qualified palmist would get the same honour as is now given to the qualified doctors. For instance, if the interview panel selecting officers be also consisting of a palmist, looking at the aspirants hand, he can know as to which job suits him best : the touring one, the administrative or the table one or the candidate may be best suited for a planning job, or for a Public Relation job.

Between the two students clearing their engineering degree, he will become an able engineer who has symptoms on the hand suggesting ample imaginative power.

In the Police and Military Services, particularly at the high posts, much planning acumen and imaginative power is needed. An imaginative person will assess the capacity of the retaliatory onslaught and his own defense first before launching his attack. Only then he can succeed better. And the symptoms for these qualities can be easily studied on their hands.

Moreover, if the candidate himself is versed in palmistry, seeing the panelist's hands through a cursory look can easily know as to who loves details and who wants concise, to the point answer.

Nisha : **Do you hope that then the government offices and the industrialist houses will also have a palmist on the board for selecting the personnel for their organisations ?**

Answer : If they feel that this knowledge has a scientific base, they may. Just 50 years ago the Yoga Discipline was confined to the caves of Himalaya. Now, let alone India, even the European countries have Yoga trainers in their colleges, hospitals and even in big hotels. Now we have Yoga sessions even in the jails. The same status palmistry might also acquire, then.

Nisha : Well, that would be a time consuming process. What are the immediate advantages of having this knowledge ?

Answer : Apart from the people coming to the palmist to have their problems sorted out, there are many possibilities and scopes for this knowledge.

While appointing one's private staff – the guard, driver or even domestic servants - knowing their basic nature by reading their hands through even a cursory glance - employer could give the proper employment.

A man with small – little finger with a well developed Jupiter Mount are honest but very sensitive and cautions about their honour. Hence they carry their resignation letter always in their pocket. Violent are those that have the top of their thumb formed like a mace - persons, with thick and longer little finger, aggressive Mars and Venus Mounts well developed but Mount of Jupiter suppressed, have no scruples in the matters of sex. Persons with developed Sun Mount and Jupiter Mount care a lot for what is proper and improper, what gives fame and what notoriety. Their this discernment save them from going the wrong way. Those who have Saturn and Mercury Mounts predominant on their hand are always very calculative. Bad symptoms can take them to the unrighteous way.

Persons with hard and rough palm texture are good for physical labour. But they don't accept new ideas readily. Persons with flexible palm are adjustable by nature. Those with heavy palms never say die. Those with longish palm do their work very methodically and skillfully.

These bits of general information can help the employer a lot in selecting the right person for the right job as also in getting the right associates and partners.

This kind of prior knowledge can nip in the bud many problems that might later become serious.

In case palmistry remains an occult science, this scope and these possibilities will be considerably limited. In order to widen its scope we want palmistry recognised as a scientific knowledge.

Part II
The Practical Formulae

Chapter VI

REMOVAL OF SOME MISCONCEPTIONS ABOUT PALMISTRY

I still remember my one childhood event seeing a cross on the Mount of Moon in my hand a palmist told my parents, "Water poses danger for him. Keep him always away from it." This warning made my parents such that they never permit me to either swim or to ride a boat. Even when going by the boat became rather indispensable I would always be surrounded with my other relatives and kith and kin so that their collective presence might ward off that feared danger to me.

When I grew big enough to conduct my life independently I traveled by steamers to visit many foreign countries and now crossing my 72nd year, I am very much before you hale and hearty.

While continuing my study in palmistry many secrets concerning the Mount of Moon gradually unveiled themselves before me whose gist is given below.

The Moon casts a cooling effect, so is the effect of water. The Moon rules the mind and the mind is always fickle. Even water doesn't remain stationary on its own. Perhaps due to some of these kinds of similarities a link must have been thought of between them.

Nevertheless, even some journey-related questions are also answered by concentrating on the Moon Mount. It is because in the olden times when rail or road routes were not available or developed, the normal mode of journey was travelling by ships and boats. Before the invention of the aeroplanes, the sea-route was the only way available for going to foreign countries. However, during my study of Palmistry, from my own experience I found that it is wrong to predict about journeyabroad looking only at the mount or moon. Other symptoms must also be considered. However, before considering these symptoms, let us understand what is meant by 'a foreign country'.

Some Facts Concerning What Is A Foreign Country

Before India's independence in 1947, the countries, the existing Pakistan and Bangladesh, were very much part of India. Both cities Amritsar and Lahore used to appear complimentary to each other. Many would spend their entire day in business of the day in Amritsar and would step off to Lahore by the evening to have fun and enjoyment.

Until some years after 1947, Goa and Sikkim were foreign strand for Indians. Now they are very much parts of India.

Despite being far way from the Indian mainland Andaman-Nicobar and the Laksha Dweep are India's integral parts while being much closer to its mainland, Male, Srilanka, Nepal and Bhutan are foreign countries for us.

In fact, the reason behind such division between the foreign and the native (our own) land is purely political. Now let us talk about the economic reasons in defining what is foreign and what is our native land.

There is a folk-song called *'Bidesia'* which is very popular in Bihar and Eastern U.P. Owing to the appalling economic conditions the male-folk of these regions had to go far-off from their native villages to earn their livelihood and bread. With the result, their separated wives used to sing this song *'Bidesia'* ('O Foreigner 1') to lessen their grief. To them anyone's going out of the village riding a bus or train was equivalent to going abroad.

On the other hand, there are also those globe-trotters who have their breakfast in Bombay, dinner in London. For them, even so called 'abroad' is their native country. Due to these definitions, a palmist always encounters difficulty in answering the foreign-journey related questions. The native's life style and other symptoms on the hand should also be considered apart from the Mount of Moon. This mount also reflects one's indomitable wish for change. The neighbouring Mount of Mercury should also be considered because the person with the strong Mercury's influence fails to stay long at one place.

As a matter of fact, while predicting about the foreign journeys, no reference should be made about foreign or native land since 'foreign' doesn't only mean going away from one's native place. It is better to say : "You may settle far from your birth place" to avoid such confusion. Since one's financial strength along with the will to travel also contributes in making foreign journey possible, symptoms for these should also be considered while studying the palm or hand.

The Whorls on The Fingers

In older times it was believed that he who had ten whorls on his fingertipps was bound to be a king.

The idea behind the concept of the kinghood is his unfettered supremacy. His word was deemed to be law for all subjects. May be, due to this unfettered authority the presence of 10 such signs might have been considered an asset but for ordinary person this is surely going to be a cause of some trouble.

The Reality Behind The Medical Symptom

The vertical lines on the Mount of Mercury are called the 'Medical Stigma' by the western palmists. We have seen them on the palms of many such persons who are not even slightely related to the medical field. My one close relative, a lady, has these lines. When, however, I studied her life-pattern I found her to be always experimenting with new recipe in her kitchen. More salt in the pulses would be diluted with the addition of the salt-less pulses. Split milk would be methodically converted into paneer (cottage cheese).

This example indicates that the presence of these lines on the Mount of Mercury tell of one's well developed nervous system. Whether such a person be in a scientific pursuit or in business, he would always be engaged in bringing about innovations different from the traditional ones. If in medical science, such persons would not depend upon their bookish knowledge but would try to achieve something original or a path-breaking research by their very active brain.

Some Misconceptions Concerning The Mount Of Jupiter

A developed mount of Jupiter is generally held to be an indication for the nature's becoming a high official. In fact, this represents his desire only, whether he attains this position or not would depend upon the conducive influence received from the other mounts as well.

Everyone wants to be saluted. But it must be realised that for receiving 100 salutes one has to give 10 salutes to others ! A Jupiter dominant person hates bowing before others. His desire of being the top person could be fulfilled only if the Sun and the Mercury Mounts cooperate with their conducive influence.

Some Misleading Beliefs About Palmistry In General

At times we receive calls from various newspaper offices. Some of their samples are given below :

1. Following the massive earth quakes in Kutch and Gujarat a phone call asked us to predict about the next possible earth quake's timing.

2. After the massive floods in Bihar and Orissa, we were asked whether we could predict about the floods.

3. During the recessionary phase in the share-markets we were asked to predict about the market picking up again the bullish trend.

4. On one New Year's Day the question was asked as to how would India fare that year.

These questions reveal people's ignorance about distinguishing between predictive astrology and palmistry.

In response my standard reply is that I am a palmist and not a Horoscope Examiner. The lines on the hand can reveal something about the persons' future and not about any community, caste or country's future in general. We can guide a person hurt by recession in the market as to how would he withstand the fluctuations or whether in frustration he would become a psyschic case or not.

Also, in case the native gets trapped in a flooded or earth-quake hit area, will he be able to evade himself out of that situation by his better vitality-force than others or not. This sums up our scope.

Some Questions Based On Personal Confusion

1. "My children stay abroad. Can you predict about their marriage seeing my hand ?"

2. "My husband's business is down. He doesn't believe in astrology or palmistry. Can you predict about his future examining my hand ?"

My standard reply is: seeing one's hand nothing much could be revealed about one's spouse or children. Even about the person himself not more than 70-80 percent can be revealed or just 20 percent about his intimate relations or friends. However, in the absence of that curious person, his palm-print could serve the purpose to some extent.

We hope, these facts about palmistry's scope and applicability will remove people's confusion about this knowledge.

Chapter VII

A PRACTICAL QUIZ

Nisha : Generally the other books on palmistry call that a fate line what you call the Line of Saturn. Also some books call that line Hepatica/Line of Lever which you call the Line of Mercury. Any specific reason behind this change is nomenclature in these cases ?

Answer : In fact all lines reveal about some aspects or the other concerning one's fate. Similarly, the health related questions also need the consideration of other lines and symptoms on the hand. So, calling a line the fate line or the other the line Hepatica give rise to some confusion. Hence, my adopting the safest way by calling the lines going towards the Saturn or Mercury Mounts as the line of Saturn and the Line of Mercury respectively.

Nisha : Cheiro reckons that time, to be the time of death when the Mercury Line crosses the life line. What is your opinion about it?

Answer : According to my experience the Line of Mercury reveals the quality of the nervous system of the person or his brain. A line emerging from the base of the Mount of Venus and going towards the Mount of Mercury cutting the Line of Life indicates (See *Fig.32*) that, at a particular age the native will be redeemed from his familial troubles and he would succeed in revealing his full personality. The origin of the Line of Mercury is close to the wrist and its termination, normally, is close to the Mount of Mercury. The marks of age on the Mercury Line are depicted by the scale used in marking the Line of Saturn. That is, the childhood period near the wrist and the old age near the Mount of Mercury (See *Fig. No.33*).

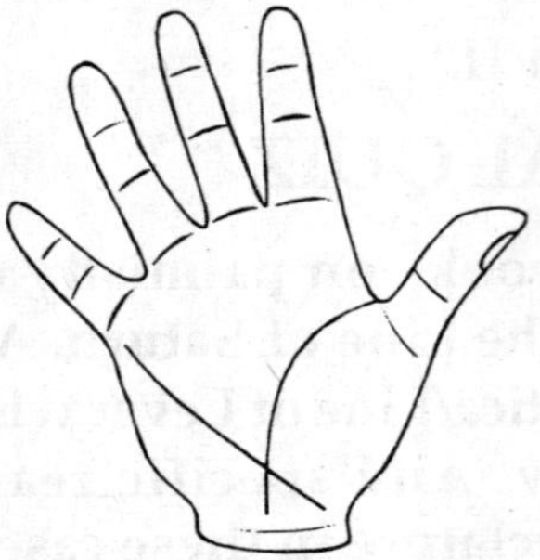

Fig. 32

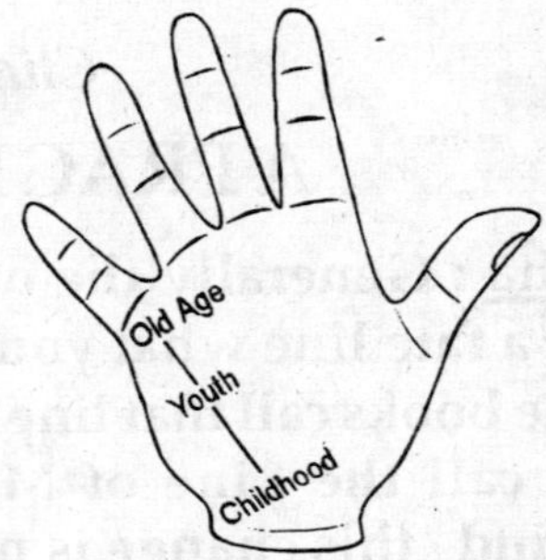

Fig. 33

This you know well that the origin of the Life Line is reckoned near the Mount of Jupiter and the middle part of the Aggressive Mars and its termination near the wrist. In other words, the childhood events are indicated at the beginning of the Life Line and the old age events at the fag-end of this line close to the wrist. (See *Fig. No. 34*)

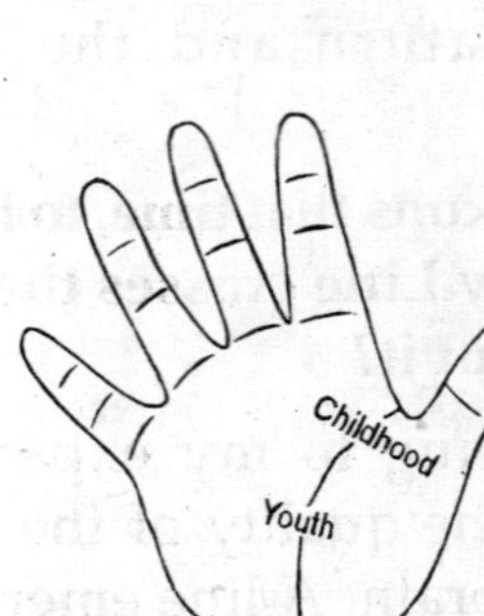

Fig. 34

I have seen in many hands that according to the Life Line scale, at 63rd year, the Mercury Line, cutting the Life-Line, was seen going towards its own mount (See *Fig. No. 35*) and the person, by the time I saw his hand, had passed 70 years of his life. According to the life-line scale measured on the Life Line that was at his age 21 years (Please see again Fig. No. 35). The person admitted his earning big profit in his business during his 21st year. Having seen many such hands I have reached on this conclusion that the Line of Mercury is the line revealing one's prudence and business acumen and it is not depicting the time of line of death.

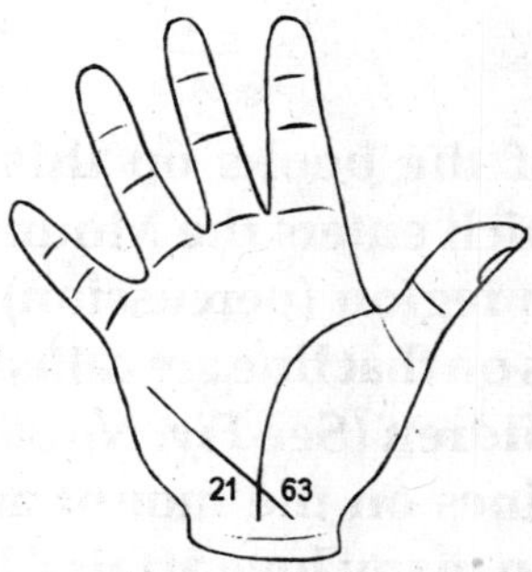

Fig. 35

<u>Nisha</u> : Which lines should be studied then for reckoning one's year or time of death, ?

<u>Answer</u> : A small or short Line of Life doesn't at all indicates less or short age of the person. Instead, by the *Life-Line scale* reckoning this should be understood that at that particular age the person will be more troubled by his family problems or he would suffer the loss of vitality at that age. In fact, supporting Mars Line at that age would augment the deficiency in the vitality (See Fig. No. 36). The lines developed with the confluence of small segments of rays or lines dispel one's vitality. Nevertheless, since predicting one's time of death is equivalent to interfering in God's work, the effort should be telling about the inauspicious symptoms as revealing damage to health. Then the remedial measures – medicines and other spiritual cures – should be suggested.

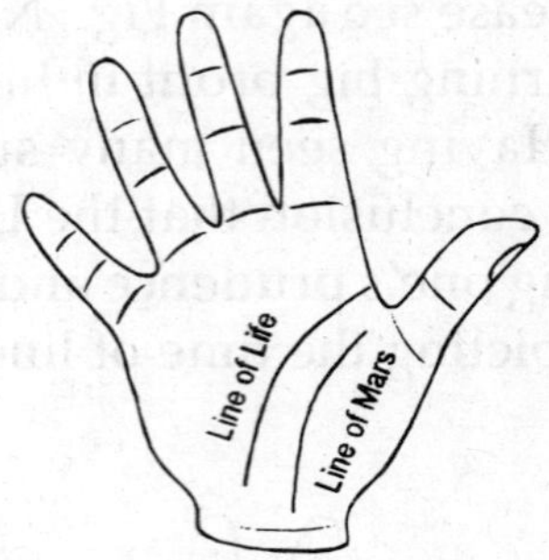

Fig. 36

Nisha : Most of the books on this subject call that marriage line which enters the Mount of Mercury from outside the palm region (percussion) (See *Fig. No. 37*). The upright lines on that line are called the progeny lines or the lines of children (See *Fig. No 38*). Also, more than one horizontal lines on the mount are called not only marriage but even many love affairs' lines. However, in your book you have called the upright lines as the lines indicative of sexual feeling and the vertical lines on the mount of Venus at the base of the thumb as the lines of children. (See *Fig. No. 39*). What is the logic behind your this conclusion.

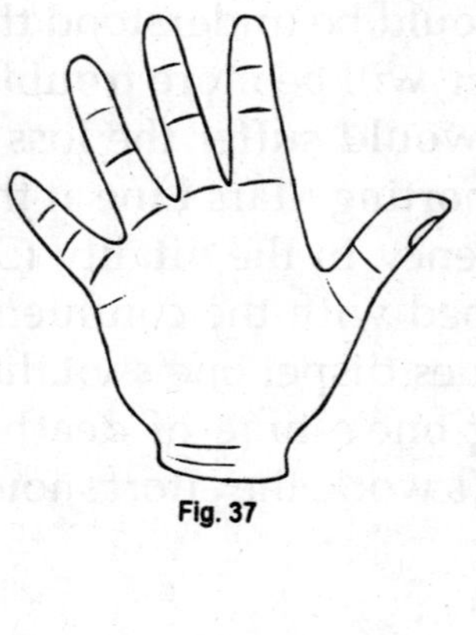
Fig. 37

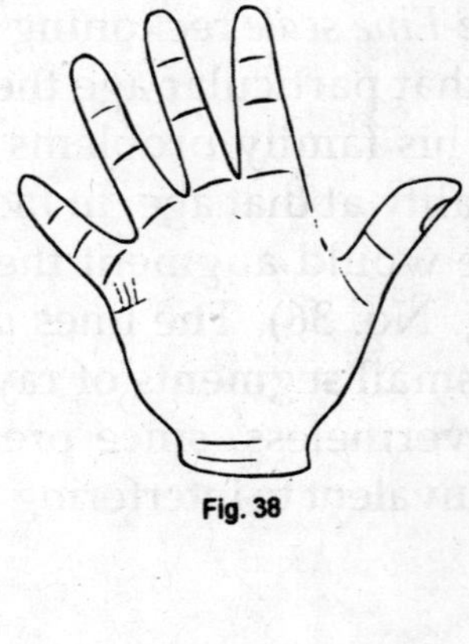
Fig. 38

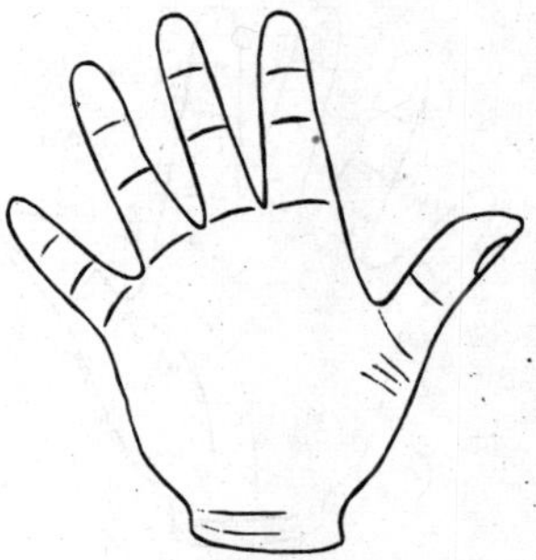

Fig. 39

Answer : The main logic is that the horizontal lines on the Mount of Mercury fail to give me the right answer concerning marriage and love-related questions. However, the other books, particularly that of ancient India gave me some indications among which the main point is reckoning the Life Line to be one's *Gotra* line as well. *Gotra* means one's lineage which is maintained by one's getting sons. The Mount of Venus represents the vitality force and the sexual feeling which arouse between the spouses or between the lover and the beloved. Since for continuation of one's lineage one needs the sexual feelings, I also gave importance to the Mars' Line, parallel to the Line of Life, in answering the marriage related question (See *Fig. No. 40*). Of course the horizontal lines on the mount of mercury do bear some indications about matrimony and after understanding them the marriage or love related questions should be tackled. But only the lines on the Mount of Mercury should not be deemed to be the sole indicative of matrimonial or love relations.

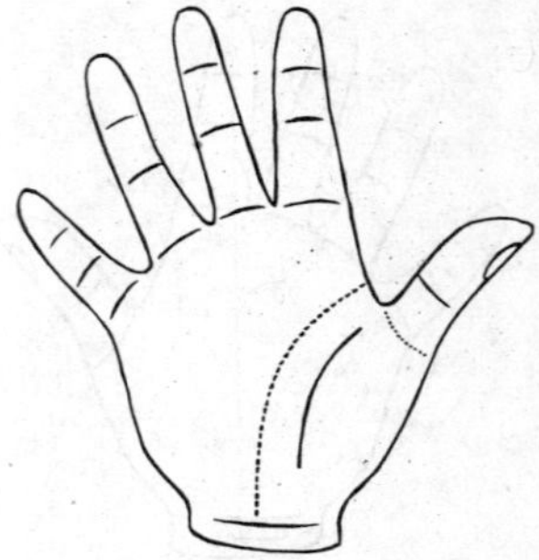

Fig. 40

According to my experience and the study that I did in this field, I find that the lines or rays ascending to the Saturn Line from the Mount of Venus and the Mount of Moon do reveal about the person's love or matrimonial life. These lines also throw light on one's partnership in other fields as well.

A long Heart Line with the fork reveals strong emotions of love. One's strong love emotion has much doubt or suspicious feelings. A man with a small Heart Line tends to have his end served by any means available.

<u>Nisha</u> : I have seen many hands having no line on the Mount of Venus, nor any Mars line. Neither, according to your theory, lines of children on the Venus Mount. But still they were married persons with children. Why is it so ?

<u>Answer</u> : It is because such persons don't care for their relations with the spouse or children. Or it can be interpreted as their having no emotional attachment with their family. They don't like to seek help from any one either as they always want to rise in life by dint of their own efforts or merit.

<u>Nisha</u> : I have also seen many hands totally devoid of the Saturn Line but they were on a very high pedestal

from the consideration of money and wealth. In sharp contrast, there are also some who have very beautifully formed Saturn Line but they were poor. How do you explain it ?

<u>Answer</u> : In fact the Saturn line indicates about the capacity or efforts for material attitude or one's material approach to life. Even the matrimonial relations are established in accordance with one's financial standing. That is why we also consider the Saturn Line while answering the marriage-related questions. Normally one succeeds in one's attempts only when the Saturn Line gets support from other conducive or helpful lines.

A parallel line of Sun or Mercury to the Line of Saturn (See *Fig. No. 41 A, B*) or the two lines' merger with the Saturn Line(See *Fig. No. 42 A, B*) gives strength to the Saturn Line. Emergence of the Sun line or Mercury Line from the Saturn Line (See *Fig. No. 43 A, B*) shows additional energy to the Saturn Line.

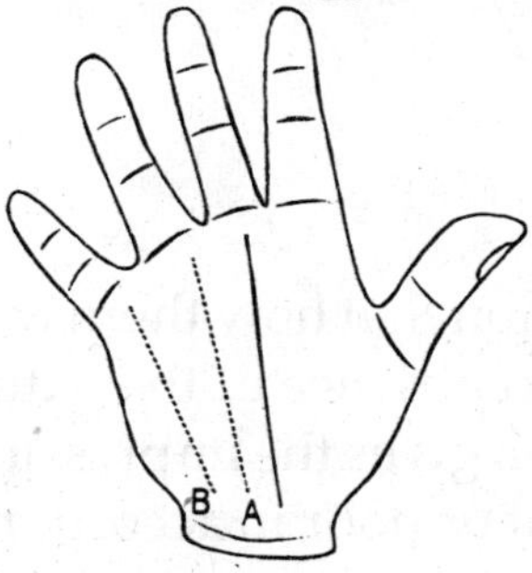

Fig. 41

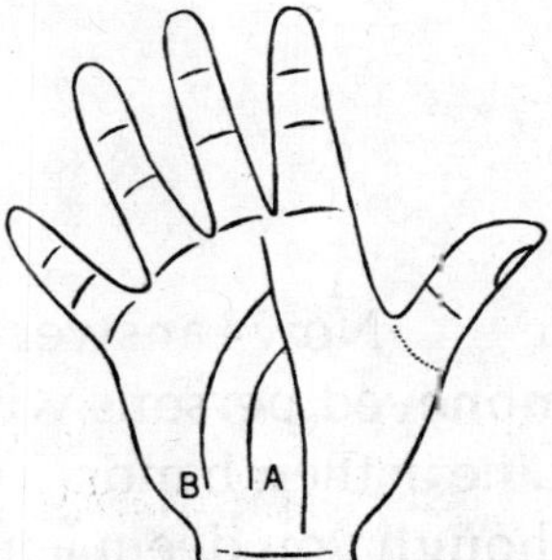

Fig. 42

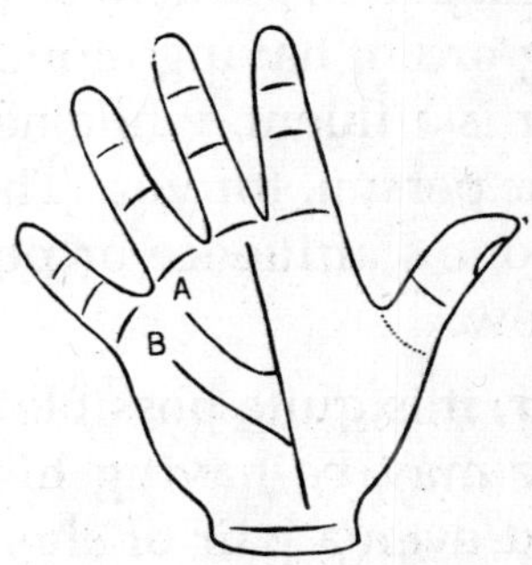

Fig. 43

The chance lines or influence lines originating from the Mount of Venus and meeting the Saturn Line or such lines originating from the Luna Mount and meeting the Saturn Line (See *Fig. No. 44 A,B*) provide strength to the Saturn Line. All these symptoms help in marriage or love related efforts to secure success eventually.

The conclusion is that the Line of Saturn indicates the efforts but this success depends on the association of this line with other conducive effect–giving lines.

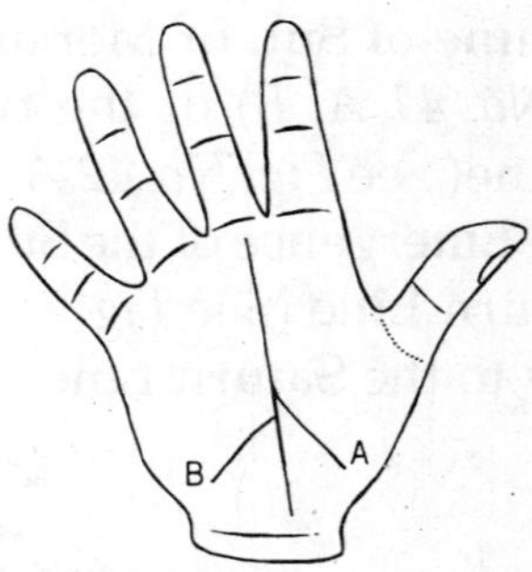

Fig. 44

Now I answer your question that how there were moneyed persons with a marked absence of the Saturn Line in their hands. Your question gives the impressions though you deem a man affluent or poor in accordance with his having or not having money respectively. He who owns a car is affluent, while he who owns only a bicycle is a poor person, for you. This is not only your scale to assess one's affluence or poverty but it is the general scale now.

However, it is quite possible that a person now owning a cycle may be having his family members unable to afford even a pair of shoes ! And he whom you saw getting down from a Maruti car might have been reared up in an atmosphere where even a Mercedes car didn't deserve any importance. Such a man may still be considering himself to be a poor person in his existing circumstances.

If a born billionaire has turned a millionaire due to his wrong decisions he is surely an unfortunate existence. Thus despite his being a millionaire his hand lines would indicate towards his poverty only.

On the other hand, there is a person who has risen high from the ghetto-level. But he becomes the owner of even a one room flat with a second hand scooter at his disposal, his hand will show indications of his constantly rising fortune.

A son or daughter of a big industrial house owns many companies even at the time of his or her birth. The right attempt to further augment his or her family property will mark his or her hand with fortunate symptoms. In case such a person makes no such attempt, the brain's electric impulses will have no contribution in the growth of his property in a routine manner. Such hands invariably don't have many lines. However, if owing to his wrong decisions his family assets decline, his hand will show unfortunate symptoms. It is, though, a different matter that his reduced family wealth may still surpass many other affluent person's economic status.

There is, however, yet another scale of measuring one's financial status. If one earns a thousand rupees, consumes Rs. 900 and leads a contented life, his hand will show the fortunate symptoms. Similarly, no matter a person's income be a crore rupees but expenditure a croce and twenty five lakhs with his sensitivity, taking this lack of resourcefulness to his heart, he will still have the unfortunate symptoms on his hand. However, if he is not much sensitive, his lines won't indicate his sorry picture. Suppose a man has to receive two crore of rupees from market but he has to pay one crore back, according to financial rules he is solvent, fortunate person. But suppose he is unable to realise his two crore rupees while he is being troubled by his creditors for returning a crore of rupees, his sensitivity will surely make his lines on the hand give adverse symptoms. But since his assets are more than his liabilities, he may soon get over his problems. The remedial measures can give him moral support till the tide actually turns favourable for him.

Remember the formula for reading the future of some one whose hand has no Saturn Line. If his Life Line be circularly moving and a part of it be below the Saturn Mount, such a Life Line in fact, has the "two in one" effect. (See *Fig. No. 45*). That is, deem that part of the Life Line going from the wrist to the Mount of Saturn to be a Line of Saturn ; from Mount of Saturn to wrist consider Line of Life (See *Fig. No. 45* and the two age-related particular years).

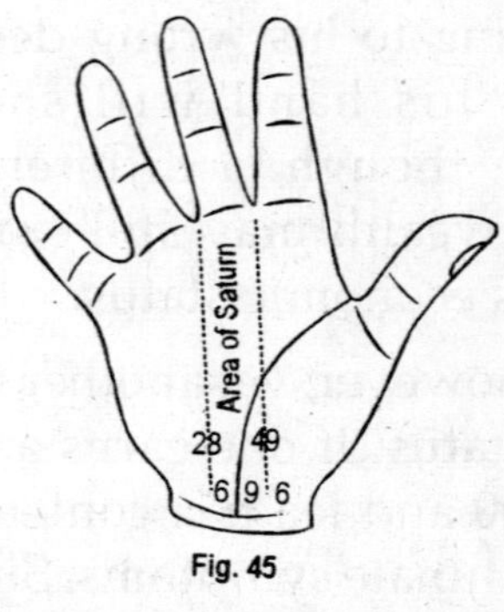

Fig. 45

If such a circularly moving Life-Line doesn't encounter any obstructive symptom, it is indicated that the native will not have many fluctuations in his life. Such persons routinely progress in a piece-meal fashion..

Some people are over-ambitious and they are never satisfied with what they gain or possess. In their case even though they may have good lines in their hand they will always be troubled by their feeling of deprivation. It becomes difficult for even a palmist to satisfy them.

Nisha : Some hands have hardly two or three lines while some have as though infinite lines like a cobweb. In either case it becomes difficult to reply their future related questions.

Answer : Less of the lines on the hand indicate that the person doesn't take any event of life with much seriousness. But even a minor most symptom on his hand will have a definite indication. In order to understand its implication his hand's all symptoms - like the mounts, built of the fingers and their length, the length and breadth of the palm, the hand's thinness or heaviness, the shape of the hand - should be studied to seek the right answer. The size and complexion of the nails, the finger prints, the texture of the skin etc., also reveal a person's innate nature which helps in searching the basic cause of the trouble. Apart from them the angle formed by the thumb when it is fully straightened also gives the clues. If the thumb thus spread forms the figure of the letter 'L' of alphabets or makes angle of 90 degree of it (See *Fig. No. 46*) with the base of the index finger, such a man is normally found to be a balanced person. If the thumb forms an acute angle, (See *Fig. No. 47*) it shows the persons tendency to stick to his guns which could be the cause of the trouble. This is also the interpretation of a person having more whorls (circle) signs on his fingertipps. However, if the angle between the spread thumb and the index finger be obtuse (See *Fig. No. 48*) it shows the person's vacillating or care-free nature. All these factors affect one's future-findings.

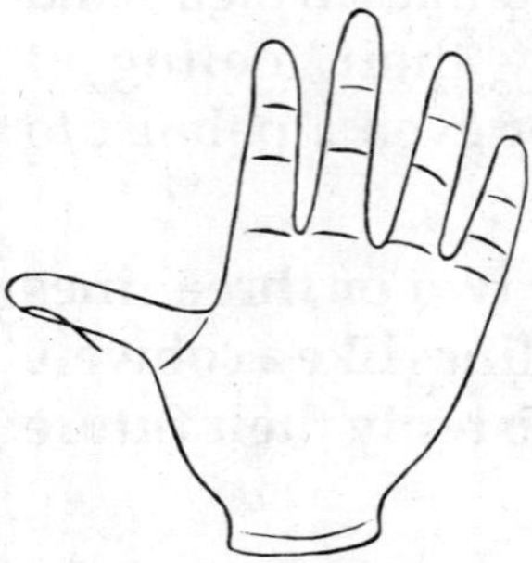

Fig. 46

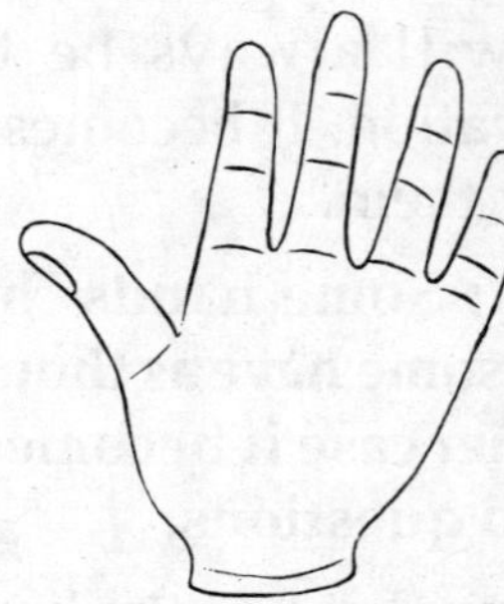

Fig. 47

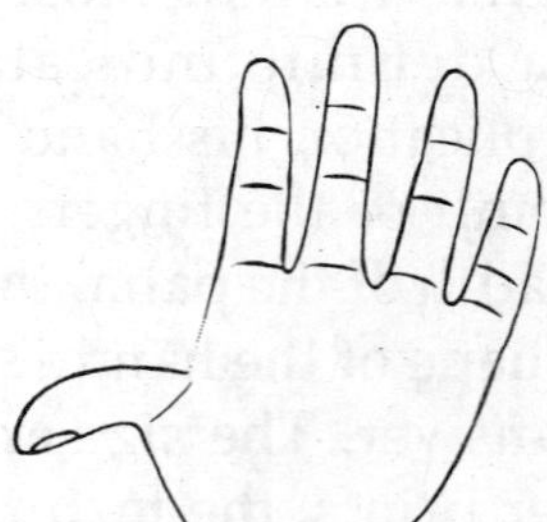

Fig. 48

If there be less distance between the fingers when they be fully spread, such persons are orthodoxical by nature. Greater distance shows the easy going nature. Either of the positions can help you assess the cause of the trouble. While learning about the basic nature from these symptoms the palmist should also suggest the remedial measures to help the person make good his deficiencies or shortcomings.

Nisha : Curiously enough, no person pleads guilty for his any wrong doing but invariably all blame their fate or their close relations, friends foes etc. Why ?

Answer : Such are the occasions when a palmist's calibre and tact in dealing with the people is put to test. He or she has to say the fact in such a way that the message may reach home but, at the same time, the person may also not feel it.

Now your question that some persons have an over abundance of lines on their palm. Persons with such hand are invariably very sensitive. Any action has its profound reaction on them. It is due to their this reaction that many chance or influence lines, coming from various directions, form many of crosses, stars, islands etc. But these signs in their hands are not as effective as on the hands with very few lines. While answering their questions, apart from the lines, other symptoms on the hand like the formation of the nails, the quality of the mounts texture, slant of the fingers and the thumb must also be considered.

Nisha : You have repeatedly referred about sensitivity in persons. Will you please elaborate on this term ?

Answer : Sensitivity means having a profound reaction to every action that one comes across. However, a person's extra sensitivity about any particular subject or topic makes him rather less sensitive in other subjects. That is, a person may be emotionally changed upon one field but he may be totally lacking emotions in other spheres. It depends upon his giving priority to specific field.

Every person has his well-marked areas of sensitivity. While one may give great priority to material wealth and position or status, the other may be very careful about one's honour. A third category of them may hold physical comforts as supreme, the fourth to sensual delights including sex; the fifth to one's familial bonds, There are also some who show great regard to their nation, caste, community or religion. He who gives extra importance to which ever these fields has his priorities guided by his marked preferences. In accordance with his top priority one becomes sensitive about it. Consequently he cares less for other preferences. But in order to preserve one's priority he may sacrifice any thing no matter what.

Normally a miserly fellow is held to be an emotion-less and those who sacrifice everything for their progeny (children) or love are said to be very emotional. I have to add only this much in this belief that even a miserly person could also be very emotional since the source of his priority lies in money or things that money can buy. So even a suggestion to his property or wealth's damage may cast a heavy impact on his head and heart. He can be a heart-patient on account of this fear.

Those that give much importance to their sexual pleasures become indifferent to their children's future and become unsympathetic to everything else.

Some, who even commit suicide fearing their name or prestige be defiled, are those that give top priority to their personal honour.

There are parents who disown their children for the sake of their community and those parents are also in existence who disown community for the sake of their children. By giving these details I want to drive home the point that sensitivity covers a wide area depending upon the individual's priority. One becomes even a psychic case when his priority is harmed due to his innate sensitivity in that field. The symptoms on the hand reveal one's such priority.

In fact, any excessive emotion in any sphere causes problems. One might be extra adventurous, extra bully-natured and overly dominating – in each case the problems originate because of one's extra sensitivity. Nevertheless, those with heavy hands never say die and they always emerge as the final victor. Till the time they have not secured the victory, they maintain their balance by following the remedial measures. Those with thin hands lose their heart very early. Such remedies should be suggested to them so as to restore their courage. The favourable symptoms appear at the marked age in the hand and that should indicate the time their desires will get fulfilled.

Nisha : You said that Saturn Line gives clues to many question's answer. It reveals about one's marriage prospects as also about business partnerships and properties etc. Other symptoms conduciveness helps one get the right answer to the queries. But how are we to know as to which line's influence or meaning should be considered when ?

Answer : When asked the same question by many students I answered it in my book entitled : "Palmistry, How To Master It". Now I repeat the same answer here also.

According to dictionary the English term 'Right' means 'towards the right side', 'correct' or the 'entitlement to do something'. One 'get' word in English could be used in scores of the ways and each time it gives us different meaning. Just as 'get away', 'get back', 'get down', 'get in', 'get on', 'get out', 'get through', 'get together', 'get up' etc. This way many examples could be cited. Every language has a particular meaning to a word in a given reference. Same way the curious person's question decides as to which meaning is to be considered when.

Nisha : But the problem is that he who comes to the palmist doesn't spell out his question in details. On the contrary he wants the palmist to guess or foretell what is his entire problem himself.

Answer : The palmists themselves are responsible for creating such a situation in the obsession of presenting themselves as some *divine* being. It is for this reason that the curious clients expect such 'foretelling' on their part.

Nevertheless, some persons are endowed with intuitive power. Could be, because of that power some of them learn what the person has in his heart. But they come into a rare and special category. Hence we are concerned with the normal practice. So while practising palmistry in a scientific way, we must clearly mark out our limits.

Nisha : Some insist on knowing before hand the colour or quality of the thing they should trade in for success - like a green, white, black or yellow coloured solid or liquid material; or whether it should be something made of iron, wood or copper etc. They also enquire as to what job in which area would suit them best. How they should be satisfied ?

Answer : The main reason for asking such question is the people's ignorance about distinguishing between palmistry and predictive astrology or the study of the horoscopes. Since I am no authority on predictive astrology I cannot intervene in this field.

However, seeing the size of the palm, the length or shape of the fingers, the knots on their fingers I can tell whether the person should be engaged in the table work or the field work; in the political field or the spiritual discipline; in the public relations' field or in the show-business. In fact the person gets the job-satisfaction as well as happiness in the field he is suited most for. It is in the chosen field that he may also get success.

While practising the scientific palmistry the curious must be told that this knowledge is a science which reveals one's hidden talent before ourself. Hence they should be asked as to which proposals they have on hand and what they want to do. They should be told clearly that by looking at their potential qualities we can tell them as to how far they can succeed in them or not. Remember that one gets success in the field that suits best one's basic nature. A man with talents in fine arts or mathematics will grow mad if forced into a contractor's job for road building. Similarly one best suited to the field work will be entangled one of his wits if employed in a table work. Hence the options for the work should come from the curious person's side. Else, aiming in the dark may or may not make one hit the target correctly.

Chapter – VIII

THE REMEDIES TO IMPROVE THE FUTURE

These remedial measures should be suggested to the person in accordance with the faith he or she adheres to. Those with longish palm, knotty long fingers are generally introvert. Those with a thin palm are also introvert. Such persons, for getting the peace of mind, resort to *Dhyana Yoga* or meditation which is the best remedy for them.

Those with broad and heavy palm are generally extrovert. The small fingers accentuate their this extrovertness. They should be advised to chant the *Mantra* of their chosen deity and to indulge in some charitable institutions.

The details about the *Dhyana Yoga, Mantras* etc. have been given by us in our book "Palmistry, How To Master It".

In order to make the various mount's influence act favourably to us, various gems studded in the ring should be used.

Nisha : Which gem or stone in the ring should be worn on which finger to ensure the favourable effect of a particular mount ?

Answer : One has to be very careful in choosing the right gem or stone in the right finger. A man with developed Mount of Jupiter and an index finger longer than the normal gets disturbed very sensitively when even a little blow is dealt on his honour. Thrown in high excitability of state he becomes incapable to take the right decision as well. In order to enhance his worldliwiseness or prudence the Mount of Mercury should be strengthened. For which wearing an emereld ring in the little finger is the right remedy.

In case a man's Mercury Mount be over-developed with the little finger thick and long, his worldliwiseness crosses the limit to become cunningness. Extra 'smartness' comes in the category of deceitfulness. Such persons fail to have any long-lasting or permanent relationship. They need their Jupiter Mount to be strengthened for which wearing Topaz in the index finger should be suggested.

The person with developed Aggressive Mars never bows before any body. On the contrary he will like to dominate over every one. Anything done against his wish is enough to rouse his anger which ruins his relations with others. But gulping down his anger may adversely effect his health. In case the Defensive Mars be developed, the person tends to gulp down his anger which aggravates his tension or depression. In order to lessen the effect of the Aggressive Mars the Mount of Saturn should be strengthened by asking him to wear an iron ring in the middle finger.

However, if the Aggressive Mars be underdeveloped or undeveloped, such a person cannot stick to his stand. He easily gives way. In order to strengthen this Mars, wearing Coral (*Moonga*) in the ring finger should be suggested. If the Defensive Mars be under developed, such a man looses his patience soon. In order to strengthen it, *Moonga* (Coral) should be worn in the ring finger.

Nisha : The reason why the gem should be worn in the ring finger to strengthen Mars is because Mars has no finger specified for it.

Answer : That is true. The gem for the mount having no specified finger should be worn in the ring finger.

Nisha : You recommend wearing an iron ring in the middle finger which is of the Saturn Mount. Normally Saturn is strengthened by suggesting the gem called Blue Sapphire or *Neelam*.

Answer : Yes ! But *Neelam* is a risky stone whereas in the use of the iron there is no risk involved. Iron also relates to Saturn and its effect is also cold.

Normally, the Mount of Saturn is generally found to be supperessed. If it be well developed with an extra long middle finger, such persons desire privacy or solitude. In order to lessen this effect a copper ring should be worn in the middle finger, because copper's eventual effect is hot which makes the person more sociable and worldliwise.

Nisha : The gem normally recommended for Venus is diamond. For an under developed Venus Mount should a person wear a diamond ring in the middle finger ?

Answer : Diamond is the gem predominantly water-oriented. The under developed Venus Mount means lack of warmth in the person. I think to make good that deficiency, coral should be recommended. If Venus be extra or over-developed, an iron ring in the ring finger will show the auspicious effect. If the Mount of Sun be under-developed with a small ring finger, to strengthen it ruby in the ring finger should be worn. In order to strengthen the Mount of Luna pearl should be worn in the ring finger.

Nisha : And if the Mount of Luna be over-developed ?

Answer : To lessen its effect *Moonga* (Coral) would be the right choice.

Nisha : Suppose a person be too poor to afford a gem. What should he or she do ?

Answer : He should wear a copper ring instead of the recommended Ruby, Topaz or Coral rings. And instead of emerald or pearl ring he should go for wearing an iron ring.

Nisha : Some astrologers recommend wearing these gems in a bracelet or necklace. What is your opinion about it ?

Answer : Well, the fingers have their direct relations with the brain centers. This fact is established because the density of the nerve-capillaries just below the end points of the finger nail is maximum, when compared with this density below any other limb of the body. Whereas, when a gem is studded in a locket or bracelet and is worn thus, it would have no direct contact with the brain. Therefore, in my opinion, it is better to wear the gems embedded in a ring. Of course for the sake of fashion a gem could be worn anywhere on the body.

Nisha : What should be the weight of a gem so recommended ?

Answer : About four to five *Rattis* (500 to 700 mg).

Nisha : Is there any especial significance of a particular day or time for wearing these gems ?

Answer : In this sphere, following the tradition is ideal. Wear the gem for strengthening the Mount of Jupiter or the index finger on Thursday; for the Saturn Mount or the middle finger on Saturday; for the Sun Mount or the ring finger on Sunday; for the entire region of Mars on Tuesday; for the Venus Mount on Friday and for the Moon Mount on Monday. The gems should be worn early in the morning.

The procedure is : say your prayers in the morning and then wear the gem. Then in every subsequent morning cast a look at that gem while praying God to grant you the right kind of wisdom. This way the psychological effect of the gem gets accentuated.

Again remember that wearing the gem with full faith in their efficacy makes them more effective. However, if one is forced to wear any gem its, effect might give contrary result.

Nisha : Why so ?

Answer : A doubting person may develop suspicion lest he be forced to wear a *Mantra*-Charged ring for subduing him totally ! Thus psychological impact can lead to many problems and hence the one wearing the gem must be duly informed in advance.